White Sox Glory

For the Love of Nellie, Shoeless Joe, and Konerko

ALAN ROSS

Cumberland House
Nashville, Tennessee

WHITE SOX GLORY
PUBLISHED BY CUMBERLAND HOUSE PUBLISHING, INC.
431 Harding Industrial Drive
Nashville, TN 37211-3160

Cover design: Gore Studio
Text design: John Mitchell
Research assistance: Ariel Robinson

Library of Congress Cataloging-in-Publication Data
Ross, Alan, 1944–
  White Sox glory : for the love of Nellie, Shoeless Joe, and Konerko / Alan Ross.
    p. cm.
  Includes bibliographical references (p. 247) and index.
  ISBN-13: 978-1-58182-535-0 (pbk. : alk. paper)
  ISBN-10: 1-58182-535-8 (pbk. : alk. paper)
  1. Chicago White Sox (Baseball team) I. Title.
  GV875.C58R67 2006
  796.357'640977311—dc22

                                                              2006000665

Printed in the United States of America

1 2 3 4 5 6 7—12 11 10 09 08 07 06

For Don Wojcik,
dear friend and top Sox fan

and for Caroline,
your courage is so inspiring,
your love so healing

"Now you know what it's like to be a waitress trying to be a singer," she said.

"If I could sing," I replied, *"I wouldn't be a writer."*

— Eliot Asinof
Bleeding Between the Lines

CONTENTS

INTRODUCTION

While talking to a dear friend from Chicago during the compilation of this book, an interesting element surfaced in conversation. Strangely, in the more than 100 years of White Sox history, not a single standout superstar rises above the legions. Sox loyalists might quickly protest on behalf of an Appling, a Minoso, a Fox, a Pierce, a Fisk, or a Thomas, but placed against the backdrop of other franchises, the point is well made. The Yankees can claim their Ruth, DiMaggio, or Mantle; the Red Sox have Ted Williams, the Cardinals Stan Musial, the Tigers Ty Cobb or Al Kaline. Even the cross-town Cubs boast the venerable Ernie Banks.

Yet on closer inspection, the Chisox' three world-champion clubs each developed a tendency that more mirrors the 1972 Miami Dolphins—that famous bunch of "no names" who carved a perfect record en route to a Super Bowl VII win. They were a team. And that's the underlying theme behind the Sox' three ultimate winners:

the Hitless Wonders; the 1917 crew that won a 100 games; and now the 2005 world champions—no super standouts, just the true essence of team sports: great teams.

White Sox Glory is the story of the American League's Chicago franchise, as told through the players themselves, the managers, coaches, opponents, fans, and media. An all-time Sox nine is presented, as well as the complete rosters of all three world-championship teams. One chapter offers remembrances of the various venues, another looks at the dark days of the Black Sox scandal. Yet another spills with Sox humor.

From Big Ed to Big Klu, Shoeless Joe to Konerko, Izzy to Ozzie, and Nellie to Looie—it's Sox time.

REMEMBRANCE

Growing up in the New York City hinterland, it was difficult not to swear your allegiances to any of the three iconic major-league teams practicing baseball there during the mid-1950s.

I remember vividly that the Chicago White Sox and the Cleveland Indians were considered "the enemy" by most New York Yankees fans at the time. A particular uneasiness would sweep through Yankee Stadium when a smallish Chisox southpaw hurler wearing No. 19 would take the mound against the Yanks—Billy Pierce. He sat down some of the greatest hitters in baseball history, and while New York's Whitey Ford was called the White Sox-killer by South Siders, Pierce likewise was referred to as the Yankee-killer by Bomber fans. More often than not, thousands of the Bronx faithful were sent home crestfallen after a Pierce win (Note: Pierce held a 9–6 career victory edge over Ford in head-to-head duels).

Last spring, I got my first glimpse of the White Sox in person in more than 50 years, at Tucson

Electric Park, the Sox' home base for spring training in Arizona. I had purposely picked the game on March 18 to attend—an encounter with the crosstown Cubs. It would be festive and hopefully competitive, I thought, knowing little love is lost between the two teams' rabid fans.

I watched the Cubs tag Sox starter Orlando "El Duque" Hernandez, the former Yankees star postseason performer, for five earned runs in five innings, and a rookie right fielder named Joe Borchard clouted a two-run home run in addition to a pulling off a defensive gem—a running catch of a foul ball down the right-field foul line. In what would appear in hindsight to have been a harbinger of the outlandish and giddy season to come, the White Sox outlasted their Windy City rival, 11–9.

But it was the presence of a young family seated next to me on the grassy center-field hillside slope beyond the fence that provided high entertainment. The mother and daughter were both decked out in Cubs replica shirts, the dad and son adorned in White Sox regalia.

"How do you manage to peacefully coexist?" I asked curiously.

The mom breathed out a laugh. "It makes for a good marriage," she said of the family's internal split of loyalties. "If we can survive this, we can survive anything!"

— *A.R.*

WHITE SOX TRADITION

Could the White Sox have won this Commissioner's Trophy without a 41-year-old Venezuelan who had exactly zero managerial experience when he was offered the Sox job two seasons ago? Put it this way: Tony La Russa couldn't win one with the Sox. Nor could Chuck Tanner, Al Lopez, Jeff Torborg, Gene Lamont, Jerry Manuel, Kid Gleason, Bob Lemon, Eddie Stanky, Paul Richards, and anyone else who came after Clarence "Pants" Rowland and that 1917 team.

Gene Wojciechowski

writer, ESPN.com,
on the job done in 2005
by manager Ozzie Guillen

In 1900, despite the misgivings of James A. Hart, owner of the Chicago National League franchise, Charles A. Comiskey transferred his St. Paul franchise to Chicago's South Side. Hart finally agreed to this invasion by a minor league rival but drove a tough bargain. He won agreement that the Comiskey team would not play north of 35th Street, and he restricted it from using "Chicago" in its name. Comiskey, denied use of "Chicago," reactivated Cap Anson's old team nickname, White Stockings. The ancient and honorable nickname kindled fond memories for older Chicagoans. It helped establish the team's identity with a city that already had a great baseball heritage.

Dave Condon

author/longtime Chicago Tribune *sportswriter*

As a player, Charles A. "the Old Roman" Comiskey revolutionized play at first base and became one of the first exponents of the head-first slide, reasoning that it enabled the runner to keep an eye on the base ahead and eliminated the possibility of a broken leg. He had been a standout manager with the old St. Louis Browns, before founding the Chicago White Sox and helping to found the American League.

Dave Condon

on the White Sox founder/owner (1900–31)

❖ ❖ ❖

After the White Sox were conceived by "the Old Roman," it was his personal conquest of the City of Chicago that gave the team life.

Bill Veeck

executive/owner (1959–61, 1976–80)

With the Browns, the imaginative Comiskey applied the principles of the man in motion to the first base job. Until then it was common practice for the guardian of that spot to keep his foot anchored to the base. Comiskey ranged afield, moved back from the base, and over into the territory between him and the second baseman. This radical move created a sensation at the time. Before long all first basemen were doing it, and a job that had been suitable for the lumbering, sedentary-type athlete now called for players of agility.

Warren Brown
author

The White Stockings played the first game in American League history (April 24, 1901), an honor they would have been forced to share had the games scheduled for Baltimore, Detroit, and Philadelphia not been rained out that day. . . . The White Sox won the pennant that maiden year of the American League. Clark Griffith posted 24 victories for them and lost only seven games.

Richard Whittingham
author

An overflow crowd of more than 14,000 watched the duel with Cleveland. . . . Manager Clark Griffith assigned opening-game hurling chores to right-hander Roy "Boy Wonder" Patterson. The Boy Wonder held Cleveland to seven hits: White Sox 8, Cleveland 2!

Dave Condon
*on the White Sox' inaugural
American League game at the
old Chicago Cricket Club grounds*

The White Sox walked away with the very first American League pennant in 1901. Midway through that first decade, they won their first World Series, defeating the Cubs in 1906, four games to two, in what remains Chicago's only intra-city baseball world-championship match.

Richard Whittingham

It is often described as the greatest upset in World Series history.

Jerome Holtzman
George Vass

authors,
on the White Sox' astounding
1906 World Series conquest of
the Chicago Cubs, who had set
an all-time major-league high for
most victories in a season (116)

The White Sox set an American League record in 1906 when they won 19 consecutive games without a loss. The streak began August 2 and lasted through August 23, during which the Sox outscored their opponents 100–24. There was also a 0–0 tie. The record win streak still stands but was tied by the New York Yankees in 1947.

Richard Whittingham

❖ ❖ ❖

Like most former players, Comiskey was not a baseball romantic. . . . Comiskey was in it for the money, a tight-fisted tyrant who kept his payroll to a minimum.

Jerome Holtzman
George Vass

❖ ❖ ❖

The lean years that followed the 1919 scandal of the "Black Sox" actually broke the heart of the Old Roman.

Bill Veeck

Comiskey had his critics but few realized that he was usually two jumps ahead of everybody else. . . . I know of no man who can get at the meat of an argument more quickly than the owner of the White Sox. It is for that reason that others listen to him, whether they are partners or rivals.

John J. McGraw
*New York Giants manager
(1902–32)*

When I graduated from St. Luke's parochial school, in River Forest, Illinois, in 1926, the class prophecy was that one day I'd be a star pitcher for the White Sox.

Johnny Rigney
*pitcher (1937–42, 1946–47)/farm
director/vice president and co-
general manager (1956–58)*

FAST FACT: Rigney married the daughter of Charles A. Comiskey, Dorothy Comiskey, who became principal owner of the White Sox (1956–59).

Frank Lane's first move [as Sox GM] was to send catcher Aaron Robinson to Detroit for $10,000 and a kid lefty named Billy Pierce, who was to win 186 games in the next 13 seasons with the White Sox.

Bob Vanderberg
author

Not all of Lane's deals—and there were almost 250 of them—were master-strokes. He admitted as much when, in 1955, he traded three players to Washington to regain [centerfielder] Jim Busby who had been sacrificed three years earlier for Sam Mele.

Bob Vanderberg

Minoso and Busby were threats to steal—causing Sox fans to begin a chant of "Go! Go!" that rocked the ballpark. Soon the chant went up whenever any of the White Sox got on base. They stole 99 bases that year (1951), an unheard of figure in those days. They were now the "Go-Go Sox."

Bob Vanderberg

❖ ❖ ❖

The '50s—it was the tops. . . . It was a time when the city loved the Sox and the Sox loved the city.

Billy Pierce
pitcher (1949–61)

When Lane developed a craving for a player on another club, that player would wind up with the White Sox. And then, in many cases, after Frank had had a chance to study the player as a member of the White Sox, another craving would develop—a desire to get rid of the guy.

Bob Vanderberg

For 39 years there had been only tears. Now champagne was flowing. The Chicago White Sox were champions of the American League, champions for the first time since that lamented autumn of 1919.

Dave Condon
on the '59 White Sox

He had already angered the stuffed shirts among the Lords of Baseball by using a midget for a pinch-hitter, by bringing tightrope walkers and baseball clowns like Max Patkin and Jackie Price into the park, by staging cow-milking contests on the field, and by allowing a group of grandstand managers armed with cue cards to dictate strategy.

Bob Vanderberg

on the reputation preceding
Bill Veeck upon his arrival
as White Sox majority owner
in 1959

When you did Bill Veeck a favor and he made you a promise, he kept it. There weren't many who did.

Frank Lane

general manager (1949–55)

Veeck was really a good man to play for. He'd do things for the ballplayers other owners wouldn't do. If you won a ballgame with a home run—especially against a good club—there'd be a check for you in the locker room for $200. He'd say, "Go buy yourself a suit." He was always doing something for the athlete to make him perform better on the field. He was so appreciative. He understood your ups and downs. He'd stay with you.

Roy Sievers
first base (1960–61)

It was kinda fun to stick the pin in some stuff-shirts, and then stand aside so we didn't get hit by the hot air.

Bill Veeck
*on his outlandish promotions
and non-traditional approach
to the game*

He was a bright and brilliant guy who could speak with authority on any subject. If he were alive today he would have his own talk show in all likelihood. I see Bill Veeck as a cross between Oprah Winfrey and the John McLaughlin Group.

Bruce Levine

commentator/writer

It was always fun to go to the park, even if the club wasn't too good. There would always be something going on—somebody parachuting out of the sky or belly dancers at home plate or some crazy thing.

Eric Soderholm

third base (1977–79)

One shudders to think what would have happened if this weren't a peaceful riot.

Richard Lindberg

author/White Sox historian, on Bill Veeck's fiasco Disco Demolition promotion, July 12, 1979

The Carlton Fisk signing had earned the new ownership instant credibility and had given Sox fans and players alike new hope—hope that had been missing on the South Side for too many defeat-filled seasons.

Bob Vanderberg
*at the outset of the Jerry Reinsdorf/
Eddie Einhorn era in 1981*

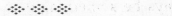

When I first came here, I was happy to be here, because it was the big leagues. All the young guys felt that way, but not the older guys. The White Sox were one team you didn't want to play for. Now, it's the place to be.

Richard Dotson
*pitcher (1979–87, 1989),
1983*

Absurd performances have been plentiful on the South Side during the last three decades. But so have brilliant ones. Grand-slam home runs served up by Gary Bell and Taylor Phillips and Don Ferrarese have been more than offset by the no-hitters of Bob Keegan and Joe Horlen. The futility of Ted Beard and Eddie McGhee as hitters has been blotted out by the awesome presence of Dick Allen and the line drives of Richie Zisk. The ineptness afield of a Ralph Garr or a Bee Bee Richard is forgotten in the remembered brilliance of an Aparicio or a Landis.

Bob Vanderberg
1984

Remember, this city is one of the founding fathers of baseball Heimlichs. Gagging noises have been heard from here, especially on the Wrigley Field side of town, for decades upon decades. Chicago children learn three dates: Columbus discovered America in 1492, the Cubs last won a World Series in 1908, the White Sox last won one in 1917.

Gene Wojciechowski

prior to the Sox' run to the world title in 2005

The White Sox are as much a part of Chicago as the wind. The Sox reflect the steelworker and the little guy fighting evil (the Yankees). They are the common man and all of his problems.

Richard Lindberg

The White Sox are known for their wacky promotions. This year they've come up with something new—winning.

Ed McGregor
writer, ESPN the Magazine,
on the 2005 world champions

THE CHISOX

Not every player with major-league talent can be a Minoso, a Thomas, or a Konerko. The everyday working fabric of White Sox baseball has always been a supportive cast of timely contributors—a Sammy Esposito, a Ken Berry, a Julio Cruz. The rosters are filled with regular heroics from the Landises, the Lollars, the Riveras, and the Rowands . . . vital cogs in the wheel, each distinctly contributing, Sox all.

Pitching with Ed Walsh in those years was a dentist/songwriter/evangelist named Doc White. The charismatic Doc's best year was 1907, when he won 27 games. Really great for a dentist!

Timothy Roberts

writer/producer

The hard luck that dogged the 1938 team did not end with the season. In November, while hunting near Greenville, Texas, Monte Stratton accidentally discharged a .32-caliber pistol, wounding himself in the right leg, piercing the femoral artery. Amputation was necessary. Though Stratton made a valiant comeback, a promising pitching career had been shattered.

Dave Condon

FAST FACT: Actor Jimmy Stewart played the lead role in the 1949 movie *The Stratton Story*.

Gus Zernial, known as "Ozark Ike," came to the Sox from the minors in 1949; the next year, his first as a regular, he promptly set a new club home-run record by belting 29.

Richard Whittingham

Alfonso Colon Carrasquel was a sensation with his glove work. This young nifty scarcely had arrived in training camp before presenting evidence that he was to displace Aches-and-Pains Appling, who in the minds of many Chicagoans had been shortstop since Ol' Ab Doubleday invented baseball. . . . His catlike fielding quickly won fans, and the *Chicago Tribune*'s Irving Vaughan, who rarely enthused about any ballplayer outside the Hall of Fame, compared him to Honus Wagner.

Dave Condon
on the Sox' shortstop from 1950 through '55

Chico Carrasquel was the league's most exciting rookie in 1950 and by '51 was outpolling the great Phil Rizzuto of New York in the All-Star balloting.

Bob Vanderberg

❖ ❖ ❖

Chico Carrasquel was almost in the same mold as Looie [Aparicio] but I didn't think he had the range Looie had. Both were so steady, and all their throws were right there. Every time.

Sammy Esposito
third base (1952, 1955–63)

❖ ❖ ❖

For seven years, Sammy Esposito was the No. 1 utility infielder in the American League. The "experts" used to say that Sammy could have been a regular with any other club in the league—except the Yankees.

Bob Vanderberg

Sherm's success was that the pitchers liked him personally—and they respected him. That's a great thing to have going for a catcher.

Al Lopez
manager (1957–65, 1968–69),
on catcher Sherman Lollar
(1952–63)

❖ ❖ ❖

He handled pitchers well; he was unflappable. Ideal, I suppose, to be employed by Lopez. You could just see these two quiet men, the old catcher and the new catcher, thinking like catchers and handling pitchers so well.

Jack Brickhouse
White Sox broadcaster (radio:
1940–43, 1945; TV: 1948–67),
on Lollar

❖ ❖ ❖

Al Lopez had told me that Sherm was like having Lopez himself out there catching. Sherm and he agreed on 95 to 99 percent of the pitches. It was like having a manager out on the field.

Bill Veeck

Ol' Jungle Jim. He had just fair ability—never a great ballplayer—but he got a lot out of it.

Marty Marion
manager (1954–56),
on Jim Rivera

That Rivera—he just played his tail off.

Jim Landis
center field (1957–64)

He was 42 years old, but he had a good arm. And he kinda liked his booze a little bit. I'll tell you one thing: when I'd call down to the bullpen to find out how he was feeling, I said, "If he's sleeping on the bench down there, and it looks like he's got a hangover, send him in." He was always good when he'd been drinking.

Marty Marion
on Ellis Kinder (1956–57)

Cool and calculating, he had ice water in his veins. He had a great sinker with good command. When he was right, they beat the ball into the ground all day long.

Ray Berres
legendary Sox pitching coach
(1949–66, 1969),
on reliever Gerry Staley

Fast Fact: It was the 39-year-old Staley's one-pitch relief appearance, on Sept. 22, 1959, at Cleveland Municipal Stadium, that brought the White Sox their first American League flag in 40 years, when he got the Indians' Vic Power to ground into a game-ending double play.

There should be a law against using Gerry Staley more than five times a week.

Frank Lane
then GM of Cleveland,
on the Sox' reliable reliever

Jim Busby, Jim Rivera, Mike Hershberger, Ken Berry—all were, at one time or another, Sox centerfielders. But none played there longer or more brilliantly than Jim Landis. He could run, he could throw, and he could catch any catchable ball—and some that were beyond the Comiskey Park bullpen fence and thus rightly judged uncatchable.

Bob Vanderberg

I always felt this: It may sound a little cocky but you had to feel this way—there was no ball I couldn't catch.

Jim Landis

You didn't want to bother him the day of the game. He'd bite your head off if you got him upset. That was the kind of intensity he put into his job. Any other day, a nicer, more congenial Irishman you'll never meet.

Jack Brickhouse
on pitcher Dick Donovan

Many people think the White Sox never would have won the pennant had it not been for the pitching of Bob Shaw. . . . There is no discounting the 18–6 record and the 2.68 earned run average Shaw, until then an unknown 25-year-old, contributed to the Chicago cause in 1959.

Bob Vanderberg

I did that because the sleeves were restricting me from swinging. They could never make a uniform for me that would give me enough room. . . . I'd get hung up. I asked them to shorten the sleeves on my uniforms, but they gave me a lot of flak. So one day, I just took a pair of scissors and cut 'em off. After a while it became kind of a symbol. It'd have to get pretty cold before I'd put a long sleeve shirt on after that.

Ted Kluszewski
first base (1959–60)

He was a hero because he could hit home runs. Roy Sievers hit 28 his first year in a Sox uniform. . . . He was also a hero because of the way he hit the Yankees.

Bob Vanderberg

Dave Debusschere would become far better known as a basketball player for the New York Knicks than he would as a pitcher for the Chicago White Sox. Nevertheless, he did wear the Sox stripes in 1962 and 1963, and won a total of three games while losing four.

Richard Whittingham

I said, "What about my hitting?" He said, "Aw, hell, you'll hit. You've hit everywhere you've played. Sometimes it just takes a little longer up here."

Pete Ward
*third base (1963–69),
on an exchange with White Sox
manager Al Lopez at the start of
Ward's rookie year in 1963. At
the time Ward was batting .211.
He finished the season at .295*

We thought he was a guy who had a chance to be a real superstar. He had tremendous power, a big strong kid, a nice boy. But it was disappointing to me—not to him—that he didn't develop the way I thought he would develop.

Al Lopez

on young slugger Dave Nicholson, who whacked 22 dingers his first season with the Sox but only totaled 15 during his final two years in Chicago

There's no super big deal about striking out, as far as I'm concerned. In the big leagues, if you walk to the plate and hit 30 groundballs to the shortstop, you may as well have struck out 30 times, 'cause you're not gonna get on base.

Dave Nicholson
outfield (1963–65)

Ken Berry—a Jim Landis-type ball-hawk—stole so many base hits out in center field that he quickly earned the nickname "The Bandit."

Bob Vanderberg

I used to practice catching home-run balls every day. If I had a situation where a ball was hit out there in batting practice, I'd go ahead and crash into the fence and jump up and see if I could catch it. Because I practiced it, I had confidence I wasn't gonna hurt myself. . . . That was my warm-up routine. Every day.

Ken Berry
center field (1962–70)

The White Sox could always count on him to throw a low-hit, low-run ballgame just about every time out. He was the American League Rookie of the Year in 1963, when he was 19–8 with a league-leading 2.33 earned run average. The next year, he was 20–8 with a 2.50 ERA.

Bob Vanderberg
on Gary Peters

FAST FACT: The athletic Peters, a one-time outfielder-first baseman candidate because he had good hitting ability, batted .259 for the Sox his rookie year of 1963 and smacked four homers and 19 RBIs in '64. For his career, he hit 19 homers. The record for most round-trippers by a pitcher is 37, by 15-year major-leaguer Wes Ferrell (1927–41).

I was a Nellie hitter—left-center and right-center. I was not a pull hitter. It helped me to wait on the ball.

Bill "Moose" Skowron
first base (1964–67)

It was a special game. Everything was just right. But I always felt I was eventually gonna throw one.

Joe Horlen
*pitcher (1961–71),
on his Sept. 10, 1967, no-hitter
against Detroit. Against
Washington in '63, Horlen had a
no-hitter going into the ninth
inning but not only lost that bid
but the ballgame as well*

Joe Horlen served as the team head-hunter. Whenever one of his teammates was brushed back by the opposition, Horlen would even it up the next inning. He would chew on his wad of tissue paper (never tobacco or gum), squirt once, and fire. The batter would go sprawling and play would resume. The fans loved it.

Rich Lindberg

I liked his bat, and we needed a bat. He could've been a real good hitter. It's too bad he blew his thumb off. He always got a piece of the ball. The way he was swinging the bat, you could tell the way he stood up there that he had confidence that he could hit. Now in the outfield, I don't think he cared if he caught the ball or not. But he could hit.

Al Lopez

on 20-year-old outfielder/ designated hitter Carlos May (1968–76), batting .281 with 18 home runs, before losing a thumb in a mortar accident at summer Marine Reserve camp

Chet Lemon hit a routine fly ball in the middle of a fog at Comiskey Park one night. The thick mist turned the usual inning-ending out into a three-run triple.

Dan Helpingstine

author,
on Lemon's bases-loaded,
first-inning fly ball to center field
against Texas on May 31, 1976,
which fell 30 feet short of the
Rangers' Tom Grieve. By the
time he retrieved the ball, the
bases had cleared and Lemon
was at third

The arrival of Julio Cruz [in 1983] turned around the infield defense and with it the pitching. All of a sudden, every ground ball hit with a man on first base was a potential double-play ball, the way the acrobatic Cruz made the pivot.

Bob Vanderberg

I would take great pleasure if I had a two-run lead and have a fastball hitter up there, and I know he's taking. I would throw a nice fastball straight down the middle. And he would just watch it go by. He'd be thinking, *How did I take that pitch?*

LaMarr Hoyt
pitcher (1979–84)

My personality as a pitcher was that I didn't mess around. It didn't bother me that I had a high ratio of hits to innings. I didn't worry about spinning a two-hitter. Just keep throwing strikes and you don't get hurt.

Jack McDowell
pitcher (1987–88, 1990–94)

On September 23, 1995, in a game at Minnesota, Lance Johnson tied a major-league record when he collected six hits in a nine-inning game. He also set a White Sox record with three triples in that game.

Richard Whittingham

Bobby Thigpen is credited with more saves than any Sox reliever in history, chalking up 201 during his eight-year career in Chicago (1986–93). The 57 he logged in 1990 is 19 more than second-ranked Roberto Hernandez. Thigpen also holds the club record for saves in a single month (13).

Richard Whittingham
1997

Rather than attract fans with his batting prowess, Belle repelled them with a surly, belligerent attitude. The Sox were glad to let him move on as a free agent to the Orioles.

Jerome Holtzman
George Vass
on Albert Belle (1997–98)

FAST FACT: The authors state that, in 1998, "a resurgent Albert Belle batted .328 and set team records with 49 home runs and 152 RBIs."

All the White Sox pitchers have taken to the quick tempo, which keeps the defense sharp. I call it the Mark Buehrle effect. He has the best reactions and most range on the staff.

Tim Keown
writer, ESPN the Magazine,
on the best of the 2005 Sox' fielding pitchers

Juan Uribe made 10 spectacular plays in September [2005]—up the middle, to the hole, coming in. He caught everything, and his throws were accurate. He fields the ball to the side, but in Latin America, that's how their heroes have always done it.

Tim Keown
Amy K. Nelson
writer/reporter, ESPN the Magazine
on the Sox' shortstop (2004–)

Bobby Jenks is 6 feet 3, 270 pounds. If he were any larger, he could rent office space.

Gene Wojciechowski
on the Sox' 2005 rookie closer

The mind and body don't always work together but when they do, Joe Crede is a complete player. He can make all the plays, and he's got a strong arm. He can even make that play coming in on the bunt and throwing on the run. When you've got a guy who can play like that and hit 22 home runs, you don't have to worry about finding a third baseman.

Tim Keown
Amy K. Nelson

❖ ❖ ❖

Joe Crede was so good that someone should have spray-painted his glove with gold paint.

Gene Wojciechowski
on the Sox' third baseman
(2000–), part of 2005's South
Side Mitt Men

Arguably the top free agent on the market, Paul Konerko, who spent the postseason putting on one heck of an audition for any team with a big bank account, is back in the fold with a five-year, $60 millon contract. And he has some new protection, coming in the form of slugger Jim Thome.

ESPN.com

This was the greatest move the White Sox could make to bring me back. I don't have many heroes, but he's one of them. He's one of the guys I've looked up to since I've been in the big leagues.

Paul Konerko
first base (1999–),
on his recent re-signing with the
White Sox plus the off-season
addition of slugger Jim Thome
from Philadelphia

Start pitching like a Cuban again.

Orlando "El Duque" Hernandez

*pitcher (2005),
to teammate/pitcher Jose
Contreras on being more
aggressive on the mound.
Contreras rebounded to go
11–2 after the 2005 All-Star
break and 3–1 in the postseason*

We planted a seed, and we loved it and watered it and took care of it every day, even though everyone told us it would never grow. And it gave us flowers and fruit. Tremendous fruit. Look at us now, eating mango.

Orlando "El Duque" Hernandez

*on helping rebuild the confidence
of friend, former teammate, and
pitcher Jose Contreras*

Scott Podsednik has almost single-handedly turned the Slo-Mo Sox into the new Go-Go Sox. His blazing speed rattles many pitchers.

Ed McGregor

I keep telling people it's because of Scott Podsednik. He bunts, steals, distracts the pitcher, and next thing you know, we have a big inning.

Mark Buehrle

pitcher (2000–),
on the secret behind the success
of the 2005 White Sox

Jermaine Dye's a smart guy and a hard worker. He's got the best arm in the outfield, and when he looks healthy, he has nice range.

Tim Keown
Amy K. Nelson

Going back on fly balls, Aaron Rowand ranks only behind Torii Hunter and Andruw Jones. He helps the corner guys by covering ground in the gaps, he has an above-average arm, and he's got no fear of the wall. He's got a football mentality; he likes to roll around and get after it.

Tim Keown
Amy K. Nelson

on the Sox center fielder
(2001–05), traded to
Philadelphia after the 2005
world-championship season

SOX CHARACTER

The saga of the White Sox was one of struggle, ingenuity, perseverance, and finally, success.

Bill Veeck

Nellie Fox in '63 took as many ground-balls as anybody who has ever played the infield. And he was near the end of his career. But he was out there working his ass off every day.

Pete Ward

In baseball, I never was scared of nothing. I thought I was like in my own home. I just went up there, knowing I had to show people.

Saturnino Orestes Arrieta Armas "Minnie" Minoso
left field (1951–57, 1960–61, 1964, 1976, 1980)

Everyone pulls for one another.

Scott Podsednik
left field (2005–)

See, when you slide with your feet first, they just wave at you with the glove and they'll call you out, if they tag you or not. So I started going in head-first all the time after that and before you know it, I liked it. And I got a lot of calls that way.

Jim Rivera
right field (1952–61)

I kind of learned a lesson in life: Don't completely inactivate yourself after being extremely active.

Bob Shaw
pitcher (1958–61)

FAST FACT: Shaw, busy with the banquet circuit and a holdout who reported late for spring training following a sensational season in 1959 (18–6, 2.68 ERA), failed to get in much physical exercise in the off-season. As a result, his numbers fell off drastically in '60. He was traded in June 1961 to Kansas City.

People can't tell you what you can be or what you can do. Only you. You're gonna have setbacks in life, but if you want something bad enough, no one can tell you that you can't have it.

Deacon Jones
infield (1962–63, 1966)

I have fought for every point because, through bitter experience, I early learned that one lost decision may mean the loss of a pennant. It is the small things in life that count; it is the inconsequential leak which empties the biggest reservoir.

Charles A. Comiskey
owner/founder (1900–1931)

You get what you earn on the field.

Paul Konerko

I had 29 pieces of glass that they took out of a cut right above my eye where my sunglasses broke. That could've ended my career right there.

Ken Berry

who during his first year smashed into Comiskey Park's center-field bullpen gate at full speed attempting to catch a home-run ball by the California Angels' Bobby Knoop. Following the incident, the White Sox padded the fence

Nothing in the world is done with talent alone, it's done with unity. My greatest strength is having the confidence to know that any of my players could do the job.

Ozzie Guillen

shortstop (1985–97)/ manager (2004–)

If a guy went 0–for–8 and we won a doubleheader, I'd expect this guy to be happy, right? And say we lost a doubleheader and he goes 7–for–8 and he's joking around the clubhouse—forget those guys. I don't want him to be laughing when we're losing and he gets his hits. To me, that's an individual-type ballplayer.

Bill Skowron

I brought a positive attitude with me. I knew the fans wouldn't take my word for it that I could hit. I had to prove myself in AA ball and do it all over again when I moved up to AAA. That's the way it is in baseball. . . . If I ever forget where I came from, I'm in trouble.

Ron Kittle
outfield (1982–86, 1989–91)

I never knocked anybody—a player, a manager, an umpire, nobody. In my own personal estimation of my career, that's the highlight: I never knocked anybody. Errors, like hits and runs, are all part of the game. Anybody can make an error.

Bob Elson

longtime radio voice of the White Sox (1930–42, 1944–70)

Keep playing like that and it'll turn. We're on the right track, I can tell.

Paul Konerko

offering a positive spin of his team's eighth loss in nine games, Freddy Garcia's one-hit loss to the Twins on Aug. 23, 2005. The AL Central's once-dominating Sox regained their footing and went on to record their third world championship

I think we'd be having fun even if we weren't doing this well.

Jon Garland
pitcher (2000–),
on the 2005 Sox

There is nothing more beautiful than being recognized and loved by your people. Trophies go away, World Series rings can even be lost, but to come to your country and receive so many sincere tokens of love is something one can never forget.

Ozzie Guillen
to the people of his native
Venezuela, who welcomed
home in early November 2005
the first Latino ever to manage
a World Series champion

SOX HUMOR

If you had 43 wives to watch, you wouldn't notice a triple play either.

Charles A. Comiskey

to a bemused bystander, when Abbas Hilmi II, Khedive of Egypt, in attendance with his 43 wives for an exhibition game between Comiskey's White Sox and John McGraw's New York Giants, apparently failed to notice a Sox triple play. The two teams had stopped in Cairo as part of their world tour in late 1913 promoting American baseball

Sooner or later, the lame, the halt, and the blind all seek refuge with us.

Bill Veeck

❖ ❖ ❖

Tommy and Joe and pray for snow.

Sox Park chant

for pitchers Tommy John and Joe Horlen, patterned after the famous "Spahn and Sain and pray for rain" doggerel that serenaded the Boston Braves' mound stars of the late 1940s

❖ ❖ ❖

Sherman Lollar was easy-going—and he ran the same way.

Jim Rivera

❖ ❖ ❖

Dad's been traded to San Francisco? Oh, boy! Now I'll get to meet Willie Mays!

Bill Pierce Jr.

whose dad was traded to the Giants following the 1961 season

That Minoso. He was something. Al Lopez or Marty Marion would bawl him out for missing a sign, and Minnie would kinda shrug his shoulders and say, "No comprendo." But if you told him, "Hey Minnie—you left a five-dollar bill on the table," he'd say, "Which table?"

Dick Donovan
pitcher (1955–60)

I used to kid and say that when I reached real far back for the good fastball that day, I'd scrape my hand on that fence.

Bob Shaw

on the 251-foot left-field fence at Los Angeles Memorial Coliseum, home of the Dodgers before Dodger Stadium at Chavez Ravine was built and the site of Games Three, Four, and Five of the 1959 World Series

Early Wynn, my roommate—I learned a lot from him, about business, about wearing mohair suits.

Bob Shaw

Frank Lane says, "Okay, Jones, I want to sign you. What do you want?" Now you've got to appreciate the fact that here I am, a young, punk kid, scared . . . and Lane's a very tough guy. I told him, "Well, I'd like to have a car." And he said, "What kind of a car do you want?" "Well, one like [Sox manager] Marty Marion's." Marty had this new black Ford convertible, and he'd only had it a week. And Lane says, "Marty, give him your car." And he did.

Deacon Jones

Gene Freese was just a ball. Just his everyday activity was a ball. He was funny. He was wild. You went out with Freese and no matter what you did or where you went, you'd have a good time. Landis was kind of a funny guy, too. Minoso was funny.

Roy Sievers

One time I was up there and hit the ball to right-center. It bounced off the fence and I rounded first base. Now a country boy, you can pull anything on them. The first baseman hollered, "Come back here!" So, I turned around and went back to first instead of getting a double.

Luke Appling
shortstop (1930–43, 1945–50)

FAST FACT: "Country boy" Appling, a seven-time AL All-Star, was from High Point, N.C.

I'd tried chewing tobacco before. I tried it 20 times and I think I threw up 20 times. That's why I started chewing Kleenex on days I was pitching.

Joe Horlen

No, my toenails didn't turn blue. My feet did, though.

Tommy John
*pitcher (1965–71),
referring to the blue sanitary
hose worn under white stirrups
by Sox players during the 1969
and '70 seasons. Some players
complained the foot covering
turned their toes blue*

He didn't trust banks. I remember one time he slid into second base and they had to hold the game up because the slide had jarred his money belt loose. He was wearing a money belt. And he had about $3,000 on him.

Jack Brickhouse
on Minnie Minoso

70

Bill Veeck's philosophy was that, while a baseball team might not give the fans a winner every day, it always could give them comfort and excitement in the park. There were strange door prizes: pigeons, cakes of ice, live chickens. There were breakfast games for war workers, with some of the stadium personnel appearing in pajamas. German bands, too. A pitcher emerged from a giant cake during one pre-game frolic.

Dave Condon

on a few of Veeck's early promotional efforts in minor-league baseball with the American Association Milwaukee Brewers, which he purchased in 1941

God must have once eaten a hamburger at Sox Park, because he is not a White Sox fan.

Rich Lindberg

It happened once in Kansas City. I thought I'd swallowed a volcano.

Nelson Fox

second base (1950–63),
asked if he had ever swallowed
his chewing tobacco

In the middle of routine conversation, Barnum Bill [Veeck] would lift up a trouser leg and snuff out a cigarette stub on an ashtray built into his artificial member.

Dave Condon

Fast Fact: Veeck had a leg amputated below the knee, a result of combat during World War II.

If there was a league in this nation that that (1976) team could have won in, it has not been brought to my attention. And that includes the Little League.

Paul Richards

manager (1951–54, 1976)

If I had my way, I'd put you in the right field stands.

> **Johnny Rigney**
>
> *to shortstop Luke Appling,*
> *who had asked Rigney, a pitcher,*
> *where he should position himself*
> *for the next batter, Ted Williams,*
> *in a 1946 game against the Red*
> *Sox. Williams then blasted "the*
> *longest home run I ever saw,"*
> *according to Rigney*

Had one fella who always dressed pretty and wore an earring. Coggins. Rich Coggins was his name. Never quite could play, but he sure did have some nice clothes.

Paul Richards

FAST FACT: Coggins, with the White Sox for the proverbial cup of coffee, played in 32 games in 1976.

Jack McDowell won the Cy Young Award in 1993 while winning 22 games. He also started the first game at New Comiskey, only to get knocked around in a 16–0 loss to Detroit. McDowell was convinced that the loss could be attributed to angering the "Gods of Old Comiskey." He and two other players burned a uniform as a sacrifice.

Dan Helpingstine

Popped it up. That wouldn't be a home run in a phone booth.

Harry Caray
*legendary play-by-play
announcer and voice of the
White Sox (1971–81),
to listeners when Sox hitters
failed in the clutch*

In a game in Cleveland a few years back, the Indians had a man on second base and one out. The batter smashed a grounder to Dick Allen, who casually grabbed the ball, stepped on first, flipped the ball to the startled umpire, and raced into the dugout (undoubtedly to catch the latest race results from Aqueduct). The umpire looked at the ball as if it would give him leprosy, and the dazed Indian runner stood on third base.

Rich Lindberg

When I walk out on the field and see all those great players, I'd better be wearing rubber pants.

Ron Kittle

admitting his awe as a rookie, in 1983, at being named to the American League All-Star Team

Smead Jolley, the legendary White Sox left fielder (1930–32), was supposed to have let a grounder roll through his legs for an error, then turned around and missed it again when the ball bounced off the wall.

Bob Logan

author/former Chicago Tribune *sportswriter*

In the late 1960s, John Justin Smith wrote a sports column for the *Daily News*. . . . He compared Sox fans to Voltaire, Rousseau, and other noble dissenters. For these indiscretions, he was exiled to the travel department of the paper, where he resided as travel editor.

Rich Lindberg

I played in a brand new pair of shoes one day and blistered my feet. The next day, I tried it with my old shoes on and just couldn't make it, so I threw away the shoes and went to the outfield in my stockinged feet. I hit a long triple in the seventh, and as I pulled into third, some guy hollered, "You shoeless sonofagun you!" They picked it up and started calling me Shoeless Joe all around the league (Carolina Association, 1908), and it stuck. I never played barefoot and that was the only day I ever played in my stockinged feet, but it stuck with me.

Shoeless Joe Jackson
left field (1915–20)

He had a collection of shoes of all types, many of them shiny patent-leather ones. The shoe fetish might have been triggered by self-consciousness over the "Shoeless Joe" label that still clung to him, a label he loathed but could not shed.

Harvey Frommer
author,
on Joe Jackson, circa 1915

❖ ❖ ❖

He was pure country, a wide-eyed, gullible yokel. It would not have surprised me in those days to learn he had made a down payment on the Brooklyn Bridge.

Joe Williams
sportswriter, New York World-Telegram and Sun, *on Shoeless Joe Jackson, 1946*

I believe that there are over 100 hits in that uniform.

Shoeless Joe Jackson
on his new road uniform, which he kept under lock and key, when he was with Cleveland prior to coming to the White Sox

Ozzie Guillen hangs out with his players. Plays golf with them. That way, he joked, "you make sure they don't talk about you. . . . The only guy who can talk about me is [Tadahito] Iguchi."

Gene Wojciechowski

> *FAST FACT:* Second baseman Iguchi is Japanese, a language Guillen does not speak.

Everyman's great moment on the Sox comes when nobody is watching.

Jean Shepherd
humorist/longtime Sox fan

I assured him if it gets passed around by drunken ballplayers after winning, it wouldn't be broken in Venezuela.

Ozzie Guillen

on his promise to Sox owner Jerry Reinsdorf that the world-championship trophy would be safe during Guillen's trip back home to Venezuela to display the prize to his countrymen

5

WHITE SOX LEGENDS

Minnie Minoso can play now. . . . In our time, you didn't get too old to play. As long as you could perform, you could play. Fay Vincent could have made something happen in 1990 when the White Sox wanted to play Minnie, and he didn't do a damn thing. That was too bad.

Nap Gulley
Negro Leagues star (Cleveland Buckeyes, Newark Eagles)

FAST FACT: Sox owner Jerry Reinsdorf claims that sourness on the part of some of the Sox' players on the '93 team killed the club's efforts to play Minoso for a record sixth decade in the major leagues.

Ed Walsh won 40 games for the White Sox in 1908, one of only two pitchers in the 20th century ever to win that many games in a single season (the other: Jack Chesbro of the New York Yankees—41 in 1904). He also set all-time White Sox records that year for number of strike-outs (269), shutouts (12), and innings pitched (464, a modern major-league record), and still posted an amazing ERA of 1.42.

Richard Whittingham

The year I won 40 games our whole club hit exactly three homers in the entire year. Fielder Jones, the manager, hit one, Frank Isbell hit another, and I got the third.

Ed Walsh
Hall of Fame pitcher (1904–16)

CHICAGO WHITE SOX

Ed Walsh

Ed Walsh's main effectiveness consists of his ability to pitch the spitball. He used a trifle of slippery elm bark in his mouth and moistened a spot an inch square between the seams of the ball. He clinched his thumb tightly lengthwise on the opposite seam, and, swinging his arm straight overhead with great force, he threw the ball straight at the plate. At times it would dart two feet down or out.

Anonymous writer
on Big Ed Walsh,
who won 17 decisions during the race to the 1906 pennant, 10 of them shutouts, three of them one-hitters. He also won two World Series games for those world-champion "Hitless Wonders"

Eddie Collins played 12 productive years with the White Sox (1915–1926) between two stints with the Philadelphia A's. One of the game's greatest hitters (lifetime average .333), Collins was also a brilliant fielder and one of the most successful base thieves in major-league history.

Richard Whittingham

During Eddie Collins's playing days an umpire—surely an unbiased observer—called him the best baseball player ever, a rather large compliment in the era of Babe Ruth, Ty Cobb, and Rogers Hornsby.

Jerome Holtzman
George Vass

He is just about the universal choice among experts as the best second baseman the AL ever had.

Jim Crusinberry
early 20th-century sportswriter,
on Eddie Collins,
1949

He was not only a natural hitter, but he had a set style, a grooved swing. I can't remember that he was ever in a batting slump. His swing was so perfect there was little chance of its ever getting disorganized.

Tris Speaker

*22-year major-league
center fielder/Hall of Famer,
on Shoeless Joe Jackson*

I used to wonder why he didn't strike out at least twice a game, taking a full cut at a ball that flopped and ducked from the treatment it got, either by emery or thumbnail or saliva.

Ty Cobb

*22-year Detroit Tigers outfielder/
Hall of Famer,
on the powerful, full swing of
Shoeless Joe Jackson*

Shoeless Joe Jackson

Ty Cobb repeatedly said Jackson was the best hitter he had ever seen. Jackson finished with a .356 career average for 13 seasons, third only behind Cobb and Rogers Hornsby.

Jerome Holtzman
George Vass

You know where Wagner's landed,
We saw where Baker's hit,
But no one ever found
The ball that Joseph Jackson hit.

Grantland Rice

legendary sportswriter,
on Jackson's monster clout off
the New York Yankees' Russell
Ford, June 4, 1913, that cleared
the Polo Grounds right-field
grandstand roof. Estimates say it
was a 500-footer. Many called it
the longest hit home run in the
majors to that time

When I was 14 I went to Sacred Heart prep school in Prairie du Chien, Wisconsin, and it was there that I began to suspect that a career on the diamond was a good way to avoid a career of milking cows. The idea grew on me when I received two dollars for pitching Sundays for the Dubuque Tigers. And I was certain of my calling when I was raised to five dollars a Sunday at 17.

Urban "Red" Faber
pitcher (1914–33)

One of the all-time great White Sox pitchers, Urban "Red" Faber was the Sox ace from 1914 through the 1920s. In Sox history, only Ted Lyons won more games.

Richard Whittingham

I liked Ted Lyons very much—he came out of Baylor University right into the big leagues and stayed. One of only four in history who did that—one was Mel Ott. Lyons was a great pitcher, a wonderful pitcher.

Bob Elson

*on the durable Hall of Famer
who pitched 21 years with the
White Sox and won 260 games,
No. 1 all-time in Sox annals*

Ted Lyons may have been the greatest pitcher ever to appear in the American League, considering his performances came during the years of the White Sox famine.

Dave Condon

*on the Chicago mound mainstay
(1923–42, 1946)*

In 1936, Luke Appling put together the longest hitting streak in White Sox history, 27 games. That year Luke also became the first White Sox player ever to win the American League batting crown. His average of .388 in 1936 remains an all-time White Sox high.

Richard Whittingham

Luke Appling became famous for fouling off pitches again and again and again and again.

Timothy Roberts

Chicago White Sox

Luke Appling

Billy Pierce, that little guy. You didn't need a relief pitcher when he was pitching. If we were a run ahead going into the seventh or eighth inning, the ballgame was over. He had more courage per ounce than any ballplayer I knew. If Pierce had been twins, we might've won it.

Frank Lane

He joined the team in 1949 and stayed on through 1961, winning 186 games—a record for Chicago lefties.

Bob Vanderberg

on Billy Pierce

I was talking to Ted Williams one day, and Williams was one of Pierce's greatest admirers.

Frank Lane

CHICAGO WHITE SOX

Billy Pierce

It was a Sunday—I'll never forget it—we had a pretty good house there, and Pierce has not pitched yet. Now, in he comes from the bullpen, this slightly built little guy, the kid they've gotten from Detroit. And now he takes a couple of warm-up pitches. On the third one he lets loose with that fastball. And you could hear an audible gasp from the crowd. He threw that fastball. Again, the gasp. Right then, boy, the chances for a star being born were there. And Billy, of course, turned out to be just that.

Jack Brickhouse
on Pierce's Comiskey Park debut in 1949

Thousands of fans loved, as I did, that little guy with the big plug of chewing tobacco in his left cheek. The little guy with the big bottle bat, the fellow who was the guts of the White Sox for so many years, the man who looped dozens and dozens of base hits into short left-center to keep countless rallies alive. . . . Nellie left behind him a record of accomplishments no White Sox second baseman will ever again approach.

Bob Vanderberg
on Nelson Fox

He always had that plug of tobacco in his cheek, and his wife, Joanne, used to bawl him out about it: "It looks terrible on television."

Billy Pierce
on Nellie Fox

CHICAGO WHITE SOX

Nellie Fox

Nellie was a tremendous competitor. He was a holler guy on the field, always giving 1,000 percent, but he was actually a quiet fellow off it. . . . He was a ballplayer who you'd say, with his size and speed, had just average talent. But what he got out of it was all-star talent. He never had the greatest arm in the world. He never had the greatest speed in the world. But he was still an all-star.

Billy Pierce

He uses a plug of tobacco per game,
and has never lost or swallowed same.
Nellie Fox so lives to play,
that every day's a hollerday.

Ogden Nash

renowned American poet

Nobody could ever throw the ball by Nellie—nobody.

Billy Pierce

Minnie Minoso was the White Sox' Jackie Robinson. Before the arrival of the Cuban Comet from Cleveland on May 1, 1951, every Chicago player had been as white as the team's sanitary socks. All white faces in white uniforms.

Bob Vanderberg

He was another of those 120 per-centers. I never saw him once complain about playing hurt. I never saw him once when he didn't give everything he had plus some more.

Jack Brickhouse
on Minnie Minoso

Minnie Minoso used to tell me that he played every game like a rookie. A rookie, he said, played each game as if he were trying to make the team.

Fausto Miranda
Miami Herald *sportswriter*

CHICAGO WHITE SOX

Minnie Minoso

Of all the players who ever played for the White Sox, and there have been some great ones, Minnie Minoso is the closest thing to a Mr. White Sox as there has been. . . . Minnie played every game as if it were the seventh game of the World Series.

Jerry Reinsdorf
owner (1981–)

Ball, bat, glove—she speak no English.

Minnie Minoso
to a reporter questioning the difficulty of Minoso playing big-league baseball with limited English

There's the ballplayer I like most to see.

Bill Veeck
on Minnie Minoso

Early Wynn's 22 wins—at the age of 39—were sensational. A few years ago I said if there was one game I absolutely had to win, Early would be my pitcher.

Al Lopez
on the Sox' mound ace during his Cy Young Award season of 1959, in which Wynn went 22–10 and pitched a league-high 256 innings

I haven't seen a shortstop yet who could top Luis Aparicio. I don't care what anybody's gonna tell me. I've played behind him too long and I've seen what he has done. And I've watched others and I still watch others. But Aparicio was fabulous.

Jim Landis

Looie, taken as a total ballplayer—considering his bat, his glove, his base running, his base stealing, his competitive spirit, the way he could take charge in a quiet way out there, the way he and Fox fit each other like a glove on the double play—it was poetry in motion. I have never seen a better shortstop than Looie.

Jack Brickhouse
on Aparicio

Zoilo Versalles, the leader of the Twins, compared himself to and styled his play after the man he idolized, Luis Aparicio.

Bill Morlock
Rick Little

authors,
on the great Sox shortstop from
1956 through '62 and from 1968
through '70

Wilbur Wood—iron man, knuckleballer, ever reliable—stepped from the bullpen to the starting rotation for the Sox in 1971. For four straight years he won 20 or more games, a Sox pitching record. Wood would bring the kind of strength and endurance to the Sox pitching of the 1970s that Big Ed Walsh had given them in the early 1900s.

Richard Whittingham

❖ ❖ ❖

The knuckleball—there's just no pattern to it, if you're throwing the ball well and if you're keeping the ball down. Once you get the ball up, it's Death Valley.

Wilbur Wood

pitcher (1967–78)

Bill Melton did a lot of things for the Chicago White Sox. I was at Comiskey Park the September night in 1970 when he did something I really believed I would never live to see a White Sox player do: His 29th homer of the year disappeared into the left-field stands, tying Gus Zernial's and Eddie Robinson's all-time club record. I thought the record would live forever. You can imagine my shock, a few days later, when Melton hit No. 30. It was a stunning message for the baseball world: There is a Chicago White Sox player capable of hitting more than 30 home runs in a single season.

Bob Vanderberg

FAST FACT: The following year, Melton's 33 round-trippers led the American League—the first time ever that a White Sox player was crowned AL home-run king.

He's one of the best players who ever played. Nobody ever played harder. . . . He's the greatest player to put on a White Sox uniform, in my opinion. Every time he went out onto the field it was like there was a big spotlight shining right on him. . . . I really believe that Dick Allen saved the Chicago White Sox franchise.

Chuck Tanner
manager (1970–75)

Dick Allen was a leader. Look at his average, .308; 37 home runs. To me, he hit about .390. For a 162-game season, Dick Allen not only hit in the clutch or stole a base, but even his outs—he just hit the ball as hard as anybody I've ever seen.

Bill Melton
on Allen's prodigious 1972 season

Everyone would like to be known as a complete ballplayer. It's not all about run, hit, throw. There's other little things to be picked up in the game that make you that good ballplayer.

Dick Allen
first base (1972–74)

The most startling event of the 1974 season occurred in September. The ever-volatile and never-predictable Dick Allen announced his retirement. At the time, he was leading the league in home runs (32) and had the top slugging average (.563). When the season ended two weeks later those figures were still the league's best. He also was batting .301. . . . The White Sox' biggest star of the '70s was suddenly extinguished.

Richard Whittingham

Ron Vesely

Harold Baines

Harold Baines would soon emerge as a true star in the American League, combining great power with high batting average and excellent run production to become one of baseball's most explosive players.

Timothy Roberts

After 10 illustrious seasons as a member of the White Sox, Harold Baines's number 3 was honorarily retired by the organization in 1989, but it had to be brought back out of retirement when he returned to the team as the designated hitter in 1996. Baines is the second-most productive home-run hitter in Sox history after Frank Thomas.

Richard Whittingham

FAST FACT: Baines's number was unretired a second time when he rejoined the club for the 2000 and 2001 seasons.

In the space of four days and two games, Carlton Fisk already had demonstrated that the White Sox made the right decision in aggressively going after him. He would remain a catching constant on the team for 12 more years even though several attempts were made to move him out. He is a Sox legend in two towns.

Dan Helpingstine

It was always fun watching Ozzie Guillen at the plate. A singles hitter, but yet a free swinger, Guillen took a hack at anything that was close. Shortstop for the 1993 division champions, Guillen began the 2004 season as Sox manager.

Dan Helpingstine

Frank Thomas, who made his debut in old Comiskey Park in 1990, holds the distinction of homering in two Comiskey Parks in two different decades.

Irving J. Cohen
author/historian

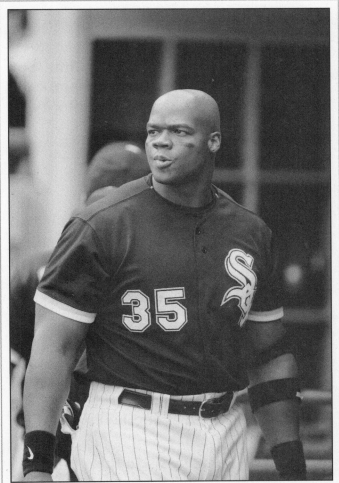

RON VESELY

Frank Thomas

Ken Harrelson, back in the White Sox broadcast booth after a two-season exile to New York, nicknamed the six-foot-five Frank Thomas "The Big Hurt."

Jerome Holtzman
George Vass

❖ ❖ ❖

Frank Thomas was the American League's MVP in 1993 and 1994, the first player in the American League to win that honor in consecutive years since Yankee Roger Maris did back in 1961–62.

Richard Whittingham

❖ ❖ ❖

Frank Thomas is the most potent offensive presence to grace a South Side diamond since Shoeless Joe Jackson—without question.

Richard Lindberg

BLACK SOX

Much like the Pocahontas narrative, the Salem witch trials, Nat Turner's slave revolt, the battle of the Alamo, the battle of Little Big Horn, the *Titanic* disaster, the bombing of Pearl Harbor, the Rosenberg espionage case, and the assassination of President Kennedy, the Black Sox scandal has successfully resisted fading into obscurity.

Daniel A. Nathan

author/assistant professor of American studies, Skidmore College

They say that Commy, the first to pay the tab and provide lavish spreads for his players, was the last to pay them fair salaries. They say, "Comiskey liked to be a big shot with the crowd, but he was cheap with his players and that's why some of them turned into Black Sox."

Dave Condon

It has often been charged that if his players had been adequately compensated, the rebellion could have been avoided. Low salaries are not an excuse, but do provide an explanation. Dropping the World Series, two weeks' work, had its appeal. The payoff would equal a year's pay.

**Jerome Holtzman
George Vass**

This, they were saying on the South Side, looked like the greatest of all White Sox teams—perhaps the greatest of all baseball teams. Playing the 1919 World Series against Cincinnati would be only a formality. The White Sox seemed certain to win in a walk.

Dave Condon

They aren't hitting. . . . The bunch I had fighting in August for the pennant would have trimmed this Cincinnati bunch without a struggle. The bunch I have now couldn't beat a high school team. . . . I tell you, I'm absolutely sick at heart. They haven't played any baseball for me.

Kid Gleason
manager (1919–23)

This most talented of all White Sox teams flopped miserably and infamously in the 1919 World Series, losing to the Cincinnati Reds, five games to three. It is the story of eight Chicago players who allegedly conspired with gamblers and agreed to throw the Series. Besides Shoeless Joe and Eddie Cicotte, first baseman Chick Gandil (the alleged ringleader), shortstop Swede Risberg, center fielder Happy Felsch, pitcher Lefty Williams, infielder Fred McMullin, and third baseman Buck Weaver were suspended from the game of baseball for life by Judge Kenesaw Landis, commissioner of baseball.

Dave Condon

It was a game of cheaters cheating cheaters, pally.

> **Abe Attell**
> *onetime world featherweight boxing champion, gambler, and key architect of the 1919 World Series fix*

It's easy. Just a slight hesitation on the player's part will let a man get to base or make a run. I did it by not putting a thing on the ball. You could have read the trademark on it, the way I lobbed it over the plate. A baby could have hit 'em. [Catcher] Ray Schalk was wise the moment I started pitching.

> **Ed Cicotte**
> *pitcher (1912–20), in his Grand Jury testimony on how he intentionally threw Game One of the 1919 World Series against Cincinnati*

Perhaps the most tragic of the eight was the popular and talented Shoeless Joe Jackson, whose remarkable career was snuffed out after batting .382 at age 31.

Timothy Roberts

Jackson's supporters claim he couldn't have been guilty because he led all Series regulars with a .375 average, set a Series record with 12 hits, and connected for the only home run. He was also errorless in the field and threw a runner out at the plate. A breakdown of the play-by-play tells a different story. In the first five games, Jackson came to bat with a total of 10 runners on base, six in scoring positions, but was inept in the clutch, failing to drive in a single run.

Jerome Holtzman
George Vass

When a Cincinnati player would bat a ball to my territory, I'd muff it if I could. But if it would too much look like crooked work to do that, I'd be slow and make a throw to the infield that would be too short. My work netted the Cincinnati team several runs that they never would have made if I'd been playing on the square.

Shoeless Joe Jackson

Only Gandil and Cicotte had shown any signs of having come into any extraordinary lot of money. Gandil had broken out with a new automobile, diamonds, and other marks of sudden affluence. Cicotte had lifted the mortgage on his home.

Warren Brown

I don't know what you'll think of me, but I double-crossed you, Mr. Comiskey. . . . I'm a crook. I got $10,000 for being a crook.

Ed Cicotte
to his boss, Comiskey, who replied, "Tell it to the grand jury"

❖ ❖ ❖

I got $5,000 and they promised me $20,000. All I got was $5,000 that Lefty Williams handed me in a dirty envelope. . . . Before I left for Cincinnati, he told me I'd get the other $15,000 after I delivered the goods. . . . Now Swede Risberg threatens to bump me off if I squawk.

Shoeless Joe Jackson

❖ ❖ ❖

The White Sox won the sixth and seventh games, and Chick Gandil testified that every man was honestly attempting to pull out the Series.

Dave Condon

During the trial as Jackson emerged from the courtroom, a young boy, the obligatory urchin, approached Shoeless Joe and, according to a September 30, 1920 report in the *Chicago Herald and Examiner*, pleaded, "Say it ain't so, Joe!" "Yes, kid, I'm afraid it is," Jackson supposedly replied.

Jerome Holtzman
George Vass

Three of the accused—Jackson, Cicotte, and Williams—signed confessions of guilt. When the confessions were "lost," the Cook County Grand Jury dismissed the charges and the players were acquitted. Nevertheless, Landis banned the eight players for life.

Jerome Holtzman
George Vass

Regardless of the verdict of juries, no player who throws a ballgame, no player who entertains proposals or promises to throw a game, no player who sits in conference with a bunch of crooked players and does not promptly tell his club about it, will ever again play professional baseball.

Judge Kenesaw Mountain Landis

✧ ✧ ✧

In addition to the eight alleged fixers, among the villains was White Sox owner Charles A. Comiskey, the so-called "Old Roman." Comiskey knew the fix was in after the first game, possibly even before.

Jerome Holtzman
George Vass

The ultimate incredibility: Joe Jackson and Ed Cicotte [who both waived immunity] were acting on the advice of counsel, the elegant Alfred Austrian— Harvard graduate, arts connoisseur, and senior partner in a prestigious Chicago law firm. But Austrian (contrary to the players' belief) was not their lawyer. He was in the service of Charles Comiskey. The Old Roman had fed his players to the grand jury to save his own skin.

James Kirby
University of Tennessee law professor

This investigation after the World Series was merely a subterfuge to fall back on in the event that the disloyalty of the ballplayers was later discovered! Comiskey accused Chick Gandil of being a ringleader immediately after the Series was over, and notwithstanding that fact, he sent him a contract for the following year!

Raymond J. Cannon
*attorney for Joe Jackson,
in Jackson's 1924 lawsuit against
Comiskey for $18,000 in back pay*

We will always wonder whether one of the accused eight went to his grave an innocent man.

Dave Condon
on Buck Weaver

Weaver was just about the best third baseman around. He never participated in the throwing of the games, or took a dime of any gambler's money, but was banished simply for his refusal to snitch on his friends. Weaver had never stopped trying to clear himself.

Eliot Asinof

author, Eight Men Out

Too bad you never got to see Buck Weaver. He really got a bad deal. He was straight all the way. The way he loved to play baseball, it was his whole life. The guy would no more throw a ballgame than murder his wife.

Urban "Red" Faber

I've thought about it plenty over the years. . . . Maybe it was one of those God-awful things that just happen to you. You don't know what you're doing, then one day you wake up and it's there, real as life. . . . We started out gabbing about all the big money we would take, like a bunch of kids pretending to be big shots. It just seemed like talk. I never really believed it would happen. I don't think any of us even wanted it to happen, 'cept Gandil. But it happened, all right. Gandil gave Cicotte ten grand the night before the opener, and the next thing we knew, we were all tied up in it.

Oscar "Happy" Felsch
center field (1915–20),
one of the Black Sox eight

They were the Black Sox. Some were blacker than others, but they all suffered. . . . They generated more sensational news than any team ever did in winning a World Series. The 1919 World Series will be replayed and reviewed when the 1959 Series is a few small-type lines in the record books. . . . Baseball never went after the fixers.

Dave Condon

❖ ❖ ❖

If the great Red Faber had been healthy enough to pitch in the 1919 Series, the greatest of all White Sox teams would have beaten Cincinnati, fix or no.

Dave Condon

❖ ❖ ❖

The Black Sox scandal is to baseball history what Benedict Arnold is to American history.

Donald Honig
historian/author

Forty years later, when the junior Bill Veeck was operating the White Sox, he discovered "Harry's Diary"—Harry Grabiner's so-called journal which had been hidden under the Comiskey Park stands. Grabiner's notes are the ultimate insider's view of the 1919 season and revealed Comiskey knew the fix was in after the first game.

Jerome Holtzman
George Vass

FAST FACT: Grabiner was the Sox' GM from 1915 through 1945.

The myth of baseball's single sin proclaims that the game has known but one case of proven dishonesty, yet the early years of the game were pockmarked with countless rumors of bribery and cheating similar to this episode.

David A. Woigt

historian,
on the Black Sox scandal

FIELD BOSSES

It's not easy to manage right now because there are a lot of players making big money, a lot of players with attitudes. The type of players I have in my clubhouse, those are the type of players that anyone can win with.

Ozzie Guillen

Clarence "Pants" Rowland, the "busher from Dubuque" who never in his life played in a major-league game, was to manage the White Sox to another world championship in 1917.

Dave Condon

FAST FACT: Rowland was the Chisox skipper from 1915 through 1918.

Jimmy Dykes was to enjoy a longer tenure than any White Sox manager and would come as close to working miracles as any mortal could. When Dykes took over, he could expect little help from the scouting system, which, according to former manager Lew Fonseca, consisted "of a man and wife combination in Texas and a San Francisco newspaperman."

Dave Condon

FAST FACT: Dykes is the winningest manager in White Sox history, racking up 894 victories from 1934 through 1946.

Paul Richards was one of the really fine baseball minds. You'd sit there and almost see the wheels go around. He had that look of the eagle—that tough Texan look about him. That wiry, leathery, muscular look. He was good. No one could reclaim pitchers better than Richards. He was another marvelous man for his time.

Jack Brickhouse

One of Paul's favorite moves was putting pitchers at third or first base so a reliever could be brought in to pitch to a certain hitter—after which the original pitcher would return to the mound to finish the game.

Bob Vanderberg

Young Mr. Paul Richards, an ambidextrous pitcher, had accomplished the believe-it-or-not feat of winning the first game of a doubleheader as a right-hander and the second as a lefty.

Dave Condon

*on the former White Sox
manager, who, as a high school
pitcher in Waxahachie, Texas,
attracted nationwide attention
for his astounding feat in the
mid-1920s*

Satisfy yourself as to what you are doing and at the same time satisfy your men that you're getting the most out of them.

Paul Richards

Al Lopez was the best manager I ever played for. In fact, he was the best manager in baseball all during my career.

Dick Donovan

❖ ❖ ❖

The transitional White Sox teams of the early to mid-1960s would not have finished nearly as high with any other manager. There is no doubt.

Richard C. Lindberg

on Al Lopez

❖ ❖ ❖

Had it not been for baseball, he said he most likely would have found his life's work in the Tampa cigar factories. That opinion, while typical of Lopez's humility, never was taken seriously by his many friends. A gentleman of Lopez's class and intelligence would have risen to prominence in any one of several fields.

Dave Condon

CHICAGO WHITE SOX

Al Lopez

Al's pet peeve was if a guy hit a fly ball and didn't hustle. That's when he would get out of his seat and be on the dugout steps waiting for you. Like Floyd Robinson. Boy, Floyd would hit a fly ball and he wouldn't run and the guy would drop the ball—and Floyd would still be at first base. Lopez would fine him $400-$500 on the spot. That was Lopez. When you loafed, he was on top of you.

Bill Skowron

Through 1959, in nine seasons as manager at Cleveland and Chicago, Al Lopez never finished lower than second!

Dave Condon

I'm proud of the record number of games I caught. Proud, too, of having caught Walter Johnson in an exhibition when I was just a kid, and of catching more than 100 games for 12 seasons, of winning the pennant at Cleveland in 1954 and at Chicago in 1959.

Al Lopez

Lopez was a lot quieter than Stanky. He wasn't perfect, though, just like Stanky wasn't perfect. He changed that lineup around an awful lot. But Al got a lot out of his players. He managed well.

Joe Horlen

He was a ballplayer's manager. If you were afraid of getting hurt or afraid of physical contact or afraid of being aggressive, then you couldn't play for Eddie. You had to love to slide, to break up double plays, to have contact with other ballplayers. That was his style. That's the way he played.

Tommy McCraw

first base (1963–70),
on Eddie Stanky, the Sox'
manager from 1966 through '68

Eddie Stanky's thinking was, if you keep the ball down to a line drive or groundball, you're gonna have to give up two or three base hits to score a run. You were better off that way than throwing up a lot of home runs or doubles and triples.

Tommy John

Stanky would do things to get guys to run through walls and do anything to win ballgames. But then he'd do things to deflate them just as fast as he had pumped them up. When you're playing 162 games in the big leagues, you have to maintain an even keel. You can't have a lot of ups and downs, because the game is as much mental as it is physical.

Anonymous starter

on one of Eddie Stanky's teams

When I was managing I could care less what your record was. I played to win a baseball game. I didn't care if you were hitting .350. If I didn't think you could hit that particular pitcher, I would take you out.

Marty Marion

When you have a curfew, the only guys you want to be strict with are the young guys. You don't want the young boys to get away with anything and start getting bad habits. Older guys you don't really worry about too much as long as they're producing.

Marty Marion

❖ ❖ ❖

My whole personality changed when I was a manager—for the worse.

Marty Marion

❖ ❖ ❖

I enjoyed managing, don't get me wrong. But the job of managing . . . your whole outlook on what you're doing personally depends on what 25 guys are doing. That's what I didn't like.

Marty Marion

When I found out I wasn't gonna be a star, I said, "Well, then, I have to have longevity." I couldn't beat out those good hitters, so I had to learn to do other things. But it wasn't until my later years that I started to assert myself on some of these things. Before that, I used to keep it to myself. I figured, "I'm not a star—nobody's gonna listen to me."

Ray Berres

responsible for developing and rejuvenating the careers of Tommy John, Ray Herbert, Bob Shaw, and Gary Peters, among others

The more I listened to him and watched him, the more I learned and the more I became an advocate of what he was teaching. As I continued on in my career, and even in coaching, I found out that the average pitching coach doesn't know what the hell he's talking about. Ray Berres, he knew what he was talking about.

Bob Shaw

on the legendary Sox pitching coach

Attitude is everything. When things were going bad, I conducted myself in the same manner as if we were winning. I walked tall, 'cause you have to walk tall. And I talked and acted positive, and I think that after a while it carried over to the ballplayers.

Chuck Tanner

When I was with the White Sox, we didn't have 25 players capable of doing the job if someone got hurt. That's why we finished where we finished.

Chuck Tanner

Every year at the end of the season we knew that we got the best out of all our ballplayers. It might have been one of the greatest jobs ever done in baseball.

Chuck Tanner

on having to play so many young players without major-league experience during his tenure with the Sox

After I left Chicago and went to Pittsburgh, it started to sink in and people have begun to realize the job we did in Chicago. They appreciated it more after we were gone.

Chuck Tanner

1981

I think you can be a nice guy and manage. A lot of guys scream and holler, but I've yet to see them win an argument.

Don Kessinger

manager (1979)

> *FAST FACT:* Kessinger lasted just 106 games piloting the White Sox.

I think we're going to find out that he is one of the really outstanding managers before he's through.

Bill Veeck

on Tony La Russa, at the outset of the manager's eight-year tenure at the Sox' helm

All I'd like is a fair shot from the fans. They can boo anything they want, but I'm going to take shots at winning wherever it makes sense. I'm not going to skip a trip to the mound to avoid one boo.

Tony La Russa

manager (1979–86)

Baseball is like putting up a building. You build and build and build until you've made a building.

Ozzie Guillen

I think Ozzie's got one of the brightest minds in baseball. The guy's only played the game since he's been able to walk.

Bo Jackson

outfielder/designated hitter (1991–93),
on former teammate and current manager Guillen

He's always done stuff to manage. I think every pitching move that was made, he was giving his two cents' worth. Plus, he's a great multi-tasker. . . . He's aware of everything.

Robin Ventura

third baseman (1989–98),
on former teammate Ozzie Guillen as Sox manager

Ozzie Guillen is the best thing to hit October since leaf blowers, hot chocolate, and Gore-Tex mittens. . . . The Ozzie Factor is visible everywhere. Nothing against Konerko, who held his newborn on Tuesday and hit a grand slam on Sunday, or Podsednik and his walk-off homer, or the nation's discovery of Joe Crede and Jenks in Game One, or the A. J. Pierzynski Immaculate Non-Reception in the American League Championship Series, or the Tony Graffanino Act of God error in the AL Division Series, but Guillen remains the centerpiece of October.

Gene Wojciechowski
on the Sox' mentor in the 2005 postseason

I think I know what you need to win.

Ozzie Guillen

I have nine other fingers on my hands that I hope to fill with World Series rings. . . . I want to be like Michael Jordan, have rings all over the place.

Ozzie Guillen

Guillen . . . seems to be the perfect combination of intuitiveness and careful study. Guillen goes by the book, but only if the book has perforated pages for easy removal. During the regular season he never used the same lineup more than three consecutive times. During the postseason he hasn't once used a different lineup.

Gene Wojciechowski

Sox fans call it Ozzie Ball. Ozzie prefers to call it Smart Ball.

Ed McGregor
on the 2005 White Sox' style of play

RON VESELY

Ozzie Guillen

We don't need superstars. We need guys who worry about the name on the chest more than the name on the back of the uniform.

Ozzie Guillen

❖ ❖ ❖

You bleed, I'm there.

Ozzie Guillen

MAJOR MOMENTS

There was one truly unforgettable game in 1984; it lasted two days. On May 8, the Sox took on the Milwaukee Brewers at Comiskey Park in a contest which was not decided until May 9 when Harold Baines finally homered in the bottom of the 25th inning to give the Sox a 7–6 victory. It stands as the longest game in major-league history, eight hours and six minutes, and the most number of innings ever in an American League game.

Richard Whittingham

In 1904, Doc White pitched five consecutive shutouts, a major-league record that would not be broken until Don Drysdale hurled six straight shutouts for the Los Angeles Dodgers in 1968.

Richard Whittingham

❖ ❖ ❖

Frank Smith hurled no-hit baseball for the White Sox on September 6, 1905, blanking the Detroit Tigers, 15–0. Three years later he would pitch another against the Philadelphia Athletics, 1–0, and become the only pitcher in Sox history to hurl two no-hit games.

Richard Whittingham

❖ ❖ ❖

Sox first basemen Frank Isbell set a World Series record in 1906 by hitting four consecutive doubles in Game Five.

Richard Whittingham

The sixth and deciding game was the only one of the Series captured by a competitor on its home grounds.

Dave Condon

on the 1906 World Series won by the White Sox' "Hitless Wonders" over their heavily favored, intra-city, National League rivals—the Cubs—four games to two. During the regular season the Cubs had set a major-league record for most victories in a season (116) that still stands to this day

Red Faber, a 16-game winner during the regular season, defeated the New York Giants three times as the White Sox won the 1917 World Series, four games to two.

Dave Condon

Ted Lyons pitched all 21 innings for the White Sox, May 24, 1929, in a single game at Detroit. The Sox lost the extra-inning affair to the Tigers, 6–5.

Richard Whittingham

The big news at Comiskey Park in 1933 occurred on July 6, when the first major-league All-Star Game was played. The game was to be a showcase for baseball's best—Frisch, Waner, Terry, O'Doul, Traynor, Gehringer, Ruth, Gehrig, Cronin, Dickey—and the game lived up to expectations. With Ruth hitting a two-run homer in the third and making a nice running catch on Chick Hafey's liner in the eighth, the American League won, 4–2, in front of more than 47,000 fans.

Bill Hageman
author

One game I'll never forget was on August 14, 1939. I pitched and won the first night game ever played in Comiskey Park.

Johnny Rigney

I was put into the lineup, batting third, against the Yankees, the world champions. Eddie Robinson, our first baseman who was batting clean-up, gave me some advice and words of encouragement before I went to the plate. On the second pitch off Vic Raschi, I hit the ball over the center field fence—what a heckuva way to start a career in Chicago.

Minnie Minoso
*on his memorable 1951
White Sox debut*

Greatest baseball fight I ever saw. Enos Slaughter picked Walt Dropo and Dropo almost killed him. There's never ever been any questioning Slaughter's courage. After all, there's a guy who's been married five times.

Jack Brickhouse

on a Yankees-Sox free-for-all in June 1957, ignited by an exchange between New York pitcher Art Ditmar and Chicago's Larry Doby after Ditmar had dusted Doby with a fastball to the head. In the ensuing melee, the Yanks' Slaughter got paired with Chicago's Dropo

On April 22, 1959, the White Sox performed a most amazing feat. They scored 11 runs in a single inning on just one hit. The deluge of runs came about as the result of 10 walks, a hit batsman, and a lone hit in the seventh inning. The Sox annihilated the Kansas City A's 20–6 that day.

Richard Whittingham

Bob Elson always called it one of the top three catches he had ever seen.

Bob Vanderberg
on Jim Landis's catch of Mickey Mantle's 460-foot blast to straightaway center field, out by the monuments in old Yankee Stadium, in 1959

Mudcat Grant was pitching for Cleveland when the White Sox came up in the sixth. Honey Romano's drive backed Jim Piersall to the center field boundary. This signaled trouble for Grant, and it came quickly. Al Smith smashed a home run over the left field wire boundary. Jungle Jim Rivera followed with a homer to right. Now the White Sox had a four-to-one edge and could hear the pennant flapping.

Dave Condon

on the White Sox' big inning in the pennant-clinching win over the Indians in '59

The magic number is none!

Bill Veeck

celebrating the White Sox' first pennant in 40 seasons—in 1959 —following Chicago's win at Cleveland, Sept. 28

That first game was my biggest thrill in baseball. It was the first Series game I'd ever been in. And I was playing. You run out onto the field and suddenly realize that this is the only game in the country and a lot of people are watching. In fact, up in the millions. I got a big thrill out of it. Even if I had had a bad Series, it still would've been the greatest moment of my life.

Ted Kluszewski

on his record-setting performance in the 1959 World Series, in which Big Klu drove in 10 runs— most ever in a six-game Series. Five of those RBIs came in Game One with a run-scoring single, and two home runs

The fifth game at L.A.—that's the biggest in memory. If you don't win it, it's all over. If you want to bring it back to Chicago, you've got to win this one. Played before the largest crowd ever to see a game in history (92,706)—it'll never be duplicated again. Fox scored a run on a double-play ball by Lollar and, by golly, they made that run stand up.

Jack Brickhouse
on the Sox' critical Game Five win at Los Angeles in the 1959 World Series

I never thought I had a chance to catch the ball. He hit the heck out of it. But I just ran as hard as I could and stuck my glove out and there it was. And we won the game 1–0.

Jim Rivera

on his 1959 World Series Game Five-winning, over-the-shoulder catch of Charley Neal's shot to right-center in the bottom of the seventh with two Los Angeles Dodgers runners aboard. Rivera's play preserved the Sox' victory, forcing a Game Six back in Chicago

On Opening Day 1960, Minnie first hit a grand-slam homer into the centerfield bullpen and then, leading off the last of the ninth, hammered a shot into the left field stands to beat Kansas City 10–9.

Bob Vanderberg

on Minoso's triumphant return to the White Sox, after spending the previous two seasons with Cleveland

The ball traveled 573 feet, eight feet farther than what had been generally accepted as the longest regular-season homer—Mickey Mantle's opening-day blast at Griffith Stadium in 1953. We had witnessed history in the making.

Bob Vanderberg

on Dave Nicholson's tape-measure blast in May 1964 against the Kansas City A's that cleared the left-field grandstand roof of Comiskey Park

I think at least 300,000 people have told me they were there.

Dave Nicholson

on his titanic round-tripper in May of 1964 against Kansas City that left Comiskey Park

On July 31, 1972, Dick Allen hit two inside-the-park home runs against the Minnesota Twins. That year, Allen became the second White Sox player to win the American League's Most Valuable Player Award. He also set the Sox all-time home-run mark for a single season that year with 37.

Richard Whittingham

If we get a couple of guys on base this inning, I'll win this for you right now.

Dick Allen

to Wilbur Wood, before the Sox went to bat in the bottom of the 21st inning of a suspended game against Cleveland in early 1973, in which Wood was the pitcher of record. Allen hitting fifth in the inning cracked a game-winning home run with two Sox on base. Wood then pitched a complete-game four-hit shutout following that game, for a doubleheader win that day

In September 1976, Bill Veeck put Minnie Minoso on the active list and Minnie went up to the plate to face California Angels pitcher Sid Monge. The Angels hadn't even existed and Monge was all of 20 days old when Minnie first stepped into that same Comiskey Park batter's box 25 years earlier. Minnie lined Monge's second pitch into left field for a single to become the oldest player in baseball history to collect a base hit. He was 53 years of age.

Bob Vanderberg

That's one game I'll probably remember the rest of my life. That was my most outstanding day in baseball.

Lamar Johnson

*first base (1974–81),
who sang "The Star Spangled
Banner" over the stadium public
address system before a June
doubleheader with Oakland in
1977. In the opener, Chicago
managed just three hits: two
home runs and a double—all by
Johnson—as the Sox won, 2–1*

A cloud of marijuana smoke hung over the stadium. It looked like a Grateful Dead concert. They couldn't have cared less about the game.

Donn Pall
pitcher (1988–93)/Sox fan in '79, on Bill Veeck's infamous Disco Demolition promotion in July 1979, in which teens brought disco records to the park as part of their admission. The records were to be destroyed between games of a doubleheader against Detroit as part of a salute to rock 'n' roll, but the ensuing chaos and unruly nature of the mostly non-baseball crowd caused the Sox to forfeit the second game. LPs flew everywhere as kids stormed the field and refused to leave

You always fantasize that a game may turn out the way it did, but you never think it is going to.

Carlton Fisk
*catcher (1981–93),
on hitting a home run in his first game with the White Sox in the season opener against his former team, Boston. Fisk's three-run eighth-inning shot put Chicago up by one en route to a 5–3 victory. In the Sox' home opener several days later, Fisk's fourth-inning grand slam propelled Chicago to a 9–3 win over Milwaukee*

Carlton Fisk, on August 17, 1990, in a game against Texas, set an all-time major-league record for home runs by a catcher, his 328th, surpassing the mark held by Hall of Famer Johnny Bench.

Richard Whittingham

RON VESELY

Carlton Fisk

Rookie outfielder Ron Kittle, like Greg Luzinski, connected in five consecutive games, and led the club in home runs with 35 and in RBIs with 100.

Jerome Holtzman
George Vass
1983

I'm stunned. This is not the way I envisioned a no-hitter. I always dreamed of getting the last out and then jumping up and down.

Andy Hawkins
New York Yankees pitcher
(1989–91),
on the oddity of July 1, 1990,
when he no-hit the Sox—and
lost! Thanks to some irregular
Yanks generosity, three errors,
two walks, and zero hits enabled
the Sox to score four runs in the
eighth inning and post a most
novel victory

Wilson Alvarez hurled a no-hitter in 1991 against the Baltimore Orioles in his first start for the White Sox and just his second in the major leagues.

Richard Whittingham

There was a delayed reaction before the crowd went wild. Some weren't sure the ball made it over the fence, and others were in awe of the magnitude of the pop-up. Bo launched the highest fly ball I have ever witnessed.

Gerry Bilek
collector/Sox fan,
on Bo Jackson's towering AL
West division-winning, three-run
clout just beyond new Comiskey
Park's left field wall, Sept. 27,
1993, in his first season back
from extensive hip-replacement
rehab

On September 4, 1995, against the Rangers in Texas, Robin Ventura tied a major-league record when he became only the eighth player in history to hit two grand slam home runs in one game. His eight RBIs also tied the club record.

Richard Whittingham

Jose Contreras's two-run, 102-pitch, $7^2/_3$-inning performance was so good it ought to have a frame around it.

Gene Wojciechowski

on the Sox' 14–2 Game One rout of Boston in the 2005 ALDS, in which Chicago sluggers belted five home runs, two by catcher A. J. Pierzynski

I know this kid is going to show up with cold blood.

> ### Ozzie Guillen
> *on Orlando "El Duque" Hernandez,*
> *summoned in relief in the sixth with the bases-loaded and no outs, protecting a one-run lead against the Red Sox in Game Three of the 2005 ALDS. Hernandez got two batters to pop up and struck out the third to help clinch the White Sox' first playoff series win since 1917*

That's the day we won the Series.

> ### Jose Contreras
> *pitcher (2004–),*
> *on Orlando "El Duque" Hernandez's masterful Game Three relief stint against Boston in the 2005 ALDS*

People think just because you've done it in the past, you're going to do it again. It's all about situations. The most important thing is to have a little bit of good luck.

Orlando "El Duque" Hernandez

who pitched scoreless, one-hit ball over three innings to preserve the White Sox' 5–3 ALDS-clinching victory over Boston in the 2005 postseason

Six pitches later Jeff Bagwell—and the would-be Astros rally—was gone, a victim of the kind of heat that lava aspires to.

Gene Wojciechowski

on reliever Bobby Jenks's performance in the eighth inning of Game One of the 2005 World Series against Houston to preserve a one-run Chicago lead, with Astros runners on second and third and two out

RON VESELY

Paul Konerko

When free agent Paul Konerko, black trench coat down, unscripted and unexpectedly reached into his pocket and handed over the last-out ball to owner Jerry Reinsdorf and he began to cry, you knew it was either the most brilliant and timely negotiation move in the history of sports, or there's a sincerity inside this organization that will not allow them to let players leave the way the Red Sox did after ending their own 86-year drought last October 28.

Scoop Jackson
journalist/author,
on a scene during the world-
champion White Sox' victory
parade through the South Side,
Oct. 28, 2005

CHICAGO WHITE SOX ALL-TIME TEAM

*L*uis Aparicio, Billy Pierce, Minnie Minoso, Eddie Collins, Dick Allen, Ted Lyons, Jim Landis, Sherman Lollar, Red Faber, Bill Melton, Ken Berry, Chico Carrasquel, Wilbur Wood . . . and these are guys who didn't make the team!

It only points out the depth of talent that the Chicago White Sox have placed on the field for well over a century. As always, tenure, that reliable benchmark of durability and consistency, merits serious weight against the prodigious marks being put up by today's young players still cresting in their careers. So, for your scrutinous review and argumentative pleasure: the Chicago White Sox All-Time Team.

Frank Thomas

First base (1990–2005)

Two-time American League MVP (1993, '94)
Five-time AL All-Star (1993–97)
AL batting champion (1997)

The Big Hurt, Frank Thomas, has virtually rewritten the slugging section of the Sox record books since he joined the ball club in 1990. Thomas is the only player in major-league history to bat .300 or better with at least 20 home runs, 100 RBIs, 100 walks, and 100 runs scored in six consecutive seasons, 1991–96, (closest to that achievement are Lou Gehrig and Ted Williams who each accomplished it, but only in four years).

Richard Whittingham

He is the greatest hitter in White Sox history.

Kenny Williams
*general manager (2001–),
on Thomas*

NELLIE FOX

Second base (1950–63)

American League MVP (1959)
Twelve-time AL All-Star (1951–61, '63)
Three-time Gold Glove Award winner (1957, '59, '60)
Hall of Fame (1997)

He was the American League's Most Valuable Player in 1959—the first Sox player to get that award. He batted .375 in the World Series that year. Twelve times he was named to the AL All-Star Team. Four times he topped the league in base hits, reaching a peak of 201 in 1954. . . . Only once did he strike out as many as 18 times in a season—that for a guy who was averaging 700 plate appearances a year.

Bob Vanderberg
on Nellie Fox

During the 1950s, Nellie Fox ruined more potential hits from his post at second base than Snooky Lanson. . . . Invariably, any second baseman who followed Fox suffered in comparison. It was like putting chateaubriand next to a quarter-pounder.

Rich Lindberg

ROBIN VENTURA

Third base (1989–98)

AL All-Star (1992)
Five-time AL Gold Glove Award winner
(1991–93, '96, '98)

I think he's the best third baseman in the league. You can count on him year in and year out. He's just an everyday player who does his job and pretty much goes unnoticed.

Alex Fernandez
pitcher (1990–96)

Remember, this is a guy who hit in 58 straight games in college. I don't care what league you're talking about, that's still two more than Joe DiMaggio.

Bobby Valentine
15-year major-league manager, on Ventura's phenomenal achievement while at Oklahoma State University

LUKE APPLING

Shortstop (1930–43, 1945–50)

Two-time American League batting champion
(1936, '43)
Seven-time AL All-Star
(1936, 1939–41, '43, 1946–47)
Retired number 4 (1975)
Hall of Fame (1964)

Luke Appling was to play more games at shortstop (2,218) than any other man in baseball history; make Comiskey Park resound with the chant "C'mon, Luke"; and, with .388 in 1936 and .328 in 1943, give the White Sox their only American League individual batting championships.

Dave Condon

Luke Appling is to the White Sox what DiMaggio was to the Yankees, Musial to the Cardinals, or Williams to the Red Sox.

Richard Whittingham

CARLTON FISK

Catcher (1981–93)

Four-time AL All-Star (1981–82, '85, '91)
Hall of Fame (2000)

The signing of Carlton Fisk changed the attitude of Chicago toward the White Sox. . . . It sent a message to people that we were for real, that it was the dawning of a new era. Carlton Fisk turned out to be that rare kind of player who plays hard because of pride. He, more than any other player we've had here, became the symbol of a new era.

Jerry Reinsdorf

Catcher Carlton Fisk was truly the White Sox man of the '80s. When he ended his baseball career after 1,421 games in a White Sox uniform, he held the Sox career home run record with 214 [since surpassed by Frank Thomas and Harold Baines].

Richard Whittingham

JOE JACKSON
Left field (1915–20)

American League leader in triples, total bases, and extra-base hits (1916)

Shoeless Joe Jackson, the most famous of those caught up in the "Black Sox" scandal, was one of the greatest hitters ever to play major-league baseball. His career batting average of .356 is third best in major-league history, exceeded only by Ty Cobb (.367) and Rogers Hornsby (.358). Shoeless Joe led the majors in triples in 1916 with 21, a White Sox team record which still stands today.

Richard Whittingham

His first year Joe Jackson hit .408. Imagine a busher doing that! And he was swinging against the dead ball, the spitball, the shine ball, and all that sort of trickery. . . . Jackson couldn't read or write, but the secret of batting was an open book to him.

Joe Williams

JOHNNY MOSTIL

Center field (1918, 1921–29)

Two-time AL leader in stolen bases (1925–26),
AL leader, runs and bases on balls (1925)

One of the finest defensive centerfielders of his day, Johnny Mostil compiled a .301 batting average in his 10 major-league seasons, all with the Sox.

Art Berke
Paul Schmitt
authors

In a spring training game played in Birmingham in 1924, the fleet-footed Mostil snared a foul fly down the left-field line—while playing center.

Richard C. Lindberg

HAROLD BAINES

Right field (1980–89, 1996–97, 2000–01)

AL leader in slugging percentage (1984)
Four-time AL All-Star (1985–87, '89)
Retired number 3 (1989);
unretired in 1996 and 2000

I admire the way he treats life as far as baseball. He has a fun time doing it, but he doesn't get overly upset by anything that happens in baseball. He realizes that it's just a game and it's your job and you do what you have to do.

Robin Ventura
on Baines

A gimpy-kneed Harold Baines in the third game of the 2000 playoffs against Seattle, hit a bloop double, advancing to third on a fly ball, and scoring on a fly to center. He barely made it both times but it was the old man's way of showing that baserunning is about more than speed, which Baines no longer had. Those little, nearly invisible things made him such a fine ballplayer.

Paul Whitfield
The South Sider

ED WALSH

Pitcher (1904–16)

Last major-league pitcher to register 40 wins
in a season (1908)
Holds major-league record for most innings
pitched, season (464 in 1908)
Career 1.82 ERA is the lowest among all
major-league pitchers since 1893
Four-time 20-game winner; Hall of Fame (1946)

There never was a pitcher Ed's equal in willingness. He'd make his regular starts and in between serve as a reliever. He actually loved to step in when trouble was on the loose. He made a ceremony of moving from the bullpen to the mound; he was one of those fellows who could strut standing still.

Irving Vaughan

Chicago Tribune *sportswriter*

Big, strong, good-looking fellow. He threw a spitball—I think that ball disintegrated on the way to the plate and the catcher put it back together again.

"Wahoo Sam" Crawford

*19-year major-league outfielder
and Hall of Famer*

AL LOPEZ
Manager (1957–65, 1968–69)

Second-winningest manager in White Sox
history (840)
American League Manager of the Year (1959)
Hall of Fame (1977)

Al Lopez sat down at the end of the bench, and there was a towel next to him. No one sat on that towel. We all said, "That's where Jesus Christ sits."

Al Smith
outfield (1958–62)

The finest manager I ever saw.

Ed Short
*general manager (1961–70),
on Al Lopez*

CHICAGO WHITE SOX ALL-TIME TEAM

Frank Thomas, *first base*

Nelson Fox, *second base*

Robin Ventura, *third base*

Luke Appling, *shortstop*

Carlton Fisk, *catcher*

Joe Jackson, *left field*

Johnny Mostil, *center field*

Harold Baines, *right field*

Ed Walsh, *pitcher*

Al Lopez, *manager*

10

THE GREAT WHITE SOX TEAMS

How good are Guillen's White Sox? This team—there are no straws that stir the Sox drink—left good behind months ago. Since then, especially once October began, they've not only flirted with greatness, they've dated it, romanced it, married it, and Wednesday evening gave birth to a bouncing, 30-pound, sterling-silver World Series championship trophy. Isn't it adorable?

Gene Wojciechowski
on the 2005 world champions

This ball club had the pop in the middle of the order to break ball games wide open, and it excelled at the hit and run game that depended on speed, smarts, and hitting behind runners. Bunting and stealing bases were additional parts of a lethal arsenal that kept the enemy guessing, wreaking havoc with speed to burn up and down the lineup.

Warren N. Wilbert
William C. Hageman

authors,
on the 1917 world-champion
White Sox

The 1917 world champions won 100 games. They never were out of first place after August 18. Happy Felsch, with .308, and Joe Jackson, with .301, led the Chicago hitters. Eddie Cicotte's 28 victories paced the hurling corps.

Dave Condon

The 1917 team was probably the closest thing to perfection that the Chicago White Sox have been able to accomplish, before or since. Unlike the 1906 team, which scratched and clawed for every run it could get, runs came easily for this ball club. They had speed, defense, hitting, and they had pitching. It was a complete solid team. They defeated the New York Giants in the World Series on a memorable play where third baseman Heinie Zimmerman chased Eddie Collins across the plate that was unguarded. As one contemporary account in the newspaper said, "the Broadway showgirls cried and the old town was just never the same when the Chicago White Sox came and defeated McGraw's Giants."

Richard Lindberg

More than any other in 1917, the scarcely recognized contribution of Dave Danforth, arguably the first outstanding southpaw relief pitcher—posting 11 wins, a .647 winning percentage, and a league-leading total of nine saves—at least in my mind, is what puts the 1917 team a notch at the head of the pack in White Sox history.

David Nemac
historian
2002

The 1919 White Sox had a star at almost every position and are regarded as one of the best teams of all-time, the equivalent of the 1927 window-breaking New York Yankees.

Jerome Holtzman
George Vass

We had a nice team. Too bad we couldn't have won it. We'd have won that thing if it hadn't been for Donovan—if ol' Tricky Dick hadn't gotten appendicitis on me.

Marty Marion

on the '55 Sox

> **Fast Fact:** Donovan was 13–4 with an ERA of 2.70 when he was felled by appendicitis on July 30, 1955. The pitcher's effectiveness fell off drastically when he attempted to return too early after the operation.

It was a combination of Frank Lane, Paul Richards, Al Lopez, astute trades, and the contributions of farm hands that enabled the Sox to climb to the American League pennant in 1959.

Bill Veeck

This has been my most fantastic season in 36 years in baseball. These fellows never gave up.

Al Lopez
on the 1959 American League-champion Chicago White Sox

When I think of that season, I think of a squibbling hit and everybody running. . . . A typical White Sox rally consisted of two bloopers, an error, a passed ball, a couple of bases on balls and, as a final crusher, a hit batsman. Never did a team make less use of the live ball.

Bill Veeck
on the '59 Sox

You can remember everybody doing something special that season. And you can remember enjoying it. . . . It was such a tremendous group of guys. You don't realize it at the time, but we had a really good ball club.

Jim Landis

on the '59 Sox

Our offense that year was Aparicio would walk and steal second, Fox would single him in, and then we'd wait three more innings.

Bill Veeck

on the Sox' offense in their 1959 AL pennant-winning year

It is remarkable that teams as generally classy as the White Sox teams of the 1950s and early '60s performed on the same field as the generally torpid, sorry crews of the late 1960s and '70s.

Bob Vanderberg

The teams that I remember here are the teams of '65, '66, '67, and '68. After that, I try to forget what happened.

Tommy John

I'm more proud of this ball club than any other club I've managed. The team is going to win a pennant next year or the year after and you are the guys who are going to win it. I'm proud of this team—so proud.

Chuck Tanner
to his 1971 White Sox

The Sox in 1972 would battle Oakland for the division title all the way into the season's final month. When the regular season was over, the Sox were in second place, only five-and-a-half games behind the A's. Their record of 87–67 was the first winning season for the Sox since 1967.

Richard Whittingham

❖ ❖ ❖

When you're winning, it's great. You can't wait to get to the ballpark. You know, '67, '72, '73—and '77, when we had an awesome ball club—the season would go by so fast, you'd say, "What happened?" You wanted to start right up again because things were going so well for everyone on the ball club.

Wilbur Wood

Veeck didn't want to pay the big bucks. It hurts, 'cause we had the team in '77 that, if we'd been together in '79 or the year before that, we might've won. If he had signed the players, like me and Richie Zisk and Soderholm and the other players that got out of there, and with Lemon and Lamar Johnson, the hitting would've been there.

Oscar Gamble
outfield/designated hitter
(1977, 1985)

They put a really good team together in 1977. All we needed was just to be patient. We had young pitchers in the minor leagues who were throwing really well. We had a great offensive attack. All we had to do was keep the team intact.

Lamar Johnson

I can't believe it, I can't believe it, I can't believe it! I've never seen anything like this before. Not the crowd, not the game. The crowd is unbelievable. That game is unbelievable. We're unbelievable.

Richie Zisk
outfield (1977),
on the '77 White Sox, the
"South Side Hit Men," after they
had taken three of four games
from second-place Kansas City
in July

Coming off a third-place finish in 1982, the White Sox surged through the American League West, winning 99 games against only 63 losses, the second most victories in club history, eclipsed only by the 100 wins posted by the 1917 World Series champion Sox. At season's end, Chicago stood 20 games ahead of second-place Kansas City in the American League West, a record margin in major-league history.

Richard Whittingham

The Sox pennant winner I pitched for in 1959 had trouble scoring runs. These fellas hit the ball on the roof.

Early Wynn

*pitcher (1958–62),
on the 1983 Sox*

I think we had a bunch of midgets. We were the Smurf team. I think I was the biggest guy on the field besides Frank Thomas.

Ozzie Guillen

*on the 1990 Sox, who played
smallball to gain a 94–68 record.
The team's leading home-run
hitter (Carlton Fisk) logged just
18 round-trippers*

The 1993 season proved to be a memorable one. Bo Jackson, becoming the first major-leaguer to play with an artificial hip, led it off with a home run on his first swing of the year. Tim Raines became only the second hitter in Sox history to homer from both sides of the plate in the same game, and became the fourth top base-stealer in major-league history. Frank Thomas demolished the club home-run record held by Dick Allen, Harold Baines, and Carlton Fisk (37) by hitting 41. And the Sox took the division title, their first since 1983, by eight games with a record of 94–68.

Richard Whittingham

A lot of people didn't know about the White Sox this year. Now a lot of people know who we are. They know who Magglio Ordonez is. They know who Carlos Lee is. People can finally put faces with names. This is definitely a stepping stone for great things to come.

Ray Durham
second base (1995–2002),
on the 1994 Sox

In 2000, the White Sox astonished the baseball world by running away with an American League division title, their young team led by one of the greatest hitters in baseball history, Frank Thomas.

Jerome Holtzman
George Vass

As recently as August 1 the White Sox were so far ahead of everyone in the AL Central that you needed Mapquest to find them. They owned the best record in baseball, were 15 games ahead of second-place Cleveland, and seemingly had nothing to worry about other than perfecting their champagne-spraying technique. Since then they've had a posture problem, slumping at the exact moment the Indians became the '27 Yankees. Cleveland began shaving away the White Sox lead as though it were peach fuzz.

Gene Wojciechowski

on the near catastrophic late-season collapse of the 2005 world-champion White Sox, whose commanding AL Central lead was whittled down to a mere 1½ games before bouncing back in the final ten days of the season

We've got 25 guys pulling on the same rope. I got to credit Ozzie Guillen for that.

Scott Podsednik

on the 2005 Sox

How does a franchise, pennantless for 45 years, having survived scandal (1919 Black Sox), explosions (scoreboard, Disco Demolition), and horrendous uniforms (collars? *shorts??*), suddenly become the best team in baseball? How does a club with fewer hits than the Royals manage to lead in a record 37 games to start 2005 and reign atop the American League Central every day this season?

Ed McGregor

Here's how great the White Sox are: No playoff series lasted long enough for them to celebrate in their own clubhouse. They've popped corks at Fenway Park, Angels Stadium, and now Minute Maid Park. . . . That's a 3–0 sweep of the former defending champion Boston Red Sox, a 4–1 series win against the Los Angeles Angels, and a 4–0 sweep of the Houston Astros.

Gene Wojciechowski

on the 2005 team

Last year we had good ballplayers. Now we have a good ball club.

Ozzie Guillen

on the 2005 Sox

FIELDS
OF PLAY

The old stadium had been home to Luke Appling, Shoeless Joe Jackson, the "Go-Go Sox," the South Side Hit Men, and Winning Ugly. For many the passing of the old park was very painful even with the argument that the old park was no longer structurally safe.

Dan Helpingstine

In 1900, the White Sox were known as the "White Stockings" and their ballpark was on the old Chicago Cricket Club grounds at 39th and Wentworth.

Richard Whittingham

The White Sox' first home was the 39th Street Grounds at 39th and Wentworth. As the first decade of the 20th century drew to a close, the old wooden-bleacher stadium was proving inadequate for a growing number of fans.

Timothy Roberts

In the venerable old stadium known as Comiskey Park (the oldest park in the majors at the time, in 1990) the ball club hosted its fans every year without fail, despite world wars and punishing economic depressions, for more than eight decades, since its gates were first opened back on July 1, 1910.

Richard Whittingham

Instead of an elaborate Roman-style façade, the Old Roman settled for his "C" monogram in burnt relief around the new park. The scheduled opening, on July 1, 1910, was seen as the dawning of a new age for baseball in Chicago. The public was greeted by a handsome brick-and-steel-girdered edifice. The new ballpark was indeed a magnificent structure.

Timothy Roberts

Old Comiskey Park

*F*orget the safety of the bone-white bases,
You gave us scores of damp hiding places,
Where fresh from the rounds of our little murders,
We found a purpose for the poles and girders;
Learned the value of obstructed view:
If you couldn't see cops, they couldn't see you.
So sip on a half pint, light up some reefer,
Grab that girl where your hand won't leave her.
Now the architects of the vault just south,
Made sure to leave the shadows out—
All gleaming, like new plumbing.
So it'll take some time
To model that concourse with bogs of grime
That slide us crosswise as we exit
To the end of the night our new route takes us.

Bob Chicoine

writer,
"The Other Side of Summer"
The Wrecking of Old Comiskey
Park

Comiskey Park remains a grand old man, a septuagenarian which has cradled the Sox and their fans since July 1, 1910, one that has earned a hallowed heritage. It virtually rings with baseball history.

Richard Whittingham

The beauty of Comiskey Park is subtle. It is perfectly symmetrical. There are no short porches, weird angles, or clinging vines. There is excellence in proportion and a calming reassurance that the park looks the same as it did in 1927 when Babe Ruth came calling.

Richard Lindberg
on old Comiskey Park

I love the smell of the stockyards in the evening.
You come home, crack a beer, supper's ready.
But that smell, that slaughterhouse smell!
Smells like . . . Comiskey!

Bob Chicoine

It goes back to the old days, the old school—the dugouts, the locker room, when there were the hard ballplayers.

Dave Winfield

on old Comiskey Park

It was one of the great baseball parks I ever play. This park, no matter if they tear it down, they going to be inside my mind. I'm gonna remember.

Minnie Minoso

on old Comiskey Park

You, Comiskey, when they ripped you down,
They plowed around the bases the wrong way—
From first to home to third—
Following the path of the clock,
But not the timeless circuit of feet
Sprinting opposite to the way a book is read:
Left to right . . . to its end.

Bob Chicoine

Old and new Comiskey Park, 1990

It wasn't like an ordinary baseball crowd. There wasn't the noise and bustle. The people were hushed, almost reverent, like you'd see in a church or a museum, and that carried over after we all filed into the stadium; it was like nothing I'd ever seen at a baseball game before. It was as if we'd come to say goodbye forever to a good friend. And of course, we had.

Richard Whittingham
on the last game at old Comiskey Park, Sept. 30, 1990

Kiss goodbye, you sentiment haters,
To the left-field stands
That caught 8,000 taters;
Most of them hit by the visitors.

Bob Chicoine

It was a real nice park, a real good park to play baseball.

Chico Carrasquel

on old Comiskey Park

❖ ❖ ❖

You could have waved a magic wand over the old Comiskey Park and made it brand new and in mint condition, and it still wouldn't have worked, because the economics of baseball had changed so much since 1981 when we had a $3 million payroll.

Jerry Reinsdorf

❖ ❖ ❖

Viewing the two parks next to each other,
Only a sap would say, "Son and mother."
Like a flat-top moored beside a frigate,
That's the way Roger Angell put it.

Bob Chicoine

Though old Comiskey Park was long ago reduced to rubble, Bill Veeck's exploding scoreboard, bleacher shower, and postgame fireworks remain staples at new Comiskey Park, aka U.S. Cellular Field, aka "The Cell."

Ed McGregor

Most of all, the old park will be remembered for such outstanding players as Shoeless Joe Jackson, Eddie Collins, Ray Schalk, Urban Faber, Luke Appling, Ted Lyons, Zeke Bonura, Minnie Minoso, Chico Carrasquel, Billy Pierce, Nellie Fox, Luis Aparicio, Wilbur Wood, Dick Allen, Bill Melton, Harold Baines, Ozzie Guillen and Frank Thomas.

**Jerome Holtzman
George Vass**

Fans held up signs that read, "Good-Bye, Old Friend," "Thanks for the Memories," and "Years From Now, We'll Say We Wuz Here." Tears flowed everywhere. Maybe chunks of cement were falling off of the place; maybe Comiskey was just too old. But saying goodbye was an emotional experience. In fact, some fans sneaked into the place during its demolition to sit in it one more time, just to remember.

Dan Helpingstine

of the 42,849 Sox loyalists who turned out for the final game at Comiskey Park, Sept. 30, 1990, a 2–1 victory over Seattle

12

RIVALRIES

I go back, put my hand on the rail and vault my self up. I'm gonna catch it. As I'm on the way up, I feel a shove, right in my back. It pushed me forward. The ball goes just over my glove. Home run. Cheap, but a home run. I turn around, and there's a New York cop standin' there. The cop was the guy who shoved me! Can you believe that?

Jim Rivera

on Joe Collins's sixth-inning home run at Yankee Stadium that gave New York a 4–0 lead in a crucial late-season game in 1955 eventually won by the Yankees, 5–4

When I was finally taken to a White Sox game, in 1954, it was as if my father sensed I was ready to learn an important lesson of life. . . . The game was typical of that Sox era. Chicago grabbed a 5–1 lead over the hated New York Yankees. Billy Pierce suffered a split nail on his pitching hand and left the game. Pitcher after pitcher paraded in, attempting to preserve the victory. The Yankees scored three in the eighth to make it 5–4. In the ninth, with two on and two out, Mickey Mantle slammed a Jack Harshman screwball into the centerfield bullpen for the ballgame. I learned at an early age that no Sox lead—in a ballgame or in a pennant race—was safe.

Bob Vanderberg

We were battling the Cubs for ink in the Chicago papers as much as we were battling the Yankees and the other clubs in our league.

Frank Lane

❖ ❖ ❖

1959 was great satisfaction, especially beating those Yankees. That was just like going to confession and coming out clean—beating the Yankees.

Anonymous White Sox fan

❖ ❖ ❖

I learned to hate the Yankees. Later, more teams would join the Yankees among the despised: The Minnesota Twins, the Baltimore Orioles, the Oakland A's, the Kansas City Royals.

Bob Vanderberg

The Yankees would always beat us. We'd win some games, but they would always win more than we did. Of course they always had a little bit more than we did—a little more depth. And that made all the difference in the world.

Billy Pierce

The Sox-Yankees games of the '50s will always be remembered on the South Side as maybe the most thrilling baseball games of the century. Especially the ones when Billy Pierce faced the American League's other premiere lefty of the era, Whitey Ford. Billy had an 8–6 record in head-to-head competition with Whitey, but he was always more concerned about facing the Yankee lineup than Ford.

Bob Vanderberg

We had a good ball club. Nobody ever said they beat us easy. They knew they were in a fight. Even the Yankees.

Billy Pierce

I'm happy I'll not have to look at Pierce and Saul Rogovin any more this year. That kind of pitching makes a manager old before his time.

Casey Stengel
New York Yankees manager,
after the conclusion of the final
White Sox-Yankees series in 1951

We scrapped. We gave 'em heck. But I'll tell you something. We were up against some team. And you've got to give them credit. They were the best team I ever saw in baseball. And that's the Yankees. . . . They were tough, super ballplayers. They had pitching, defense, running, everything.

Jim Rivera

The Yankees can be had.

Al Lopez

❖ ❖ ❖

Hey, whatever happened to the Yankees?

Jim Rivera
following the Sox' pennant-clinching win over Cleveland in 1959

❖ ❖ ❖

There had been 203 Cubs-White Sox exhibition games, with the Sox holding a decisive edge, 123 victories against 75 losses and five ties. From 1902 through 1942 the teams played a City Series, often in a best-of-seven format, before or after the regular season. Thereafter one game was player annually for a variety of charitable causes.

**Jerome Holtzman
George Vass**
2001

The fabled City Series was played for pride in its heyday of the 1920s and 1930s. The players wanted to win as badly as the fans—maybe even more so. And [manager] Jimmy Dykes took personal delight in sticking the needle into the side of the North Siders following fresh White Sox victories.

Richard Lindberg

❖ ❖ ❖

My grandfather grew up with the Black Sox. He told me, "You are a White Sox fan." He also told me that I would hate the Cubs.

Anonymous White Sox fan

❖ ❖ ❖

A baseball "war" has raged for more than 100 years and can never end, given the natural allegiance and antipathy of Cub and White Sox fans.

Jerome Holtzman
George Vass

Less than 10 miles separate Wrigley from U.S. Cellular Field, but it might as well be the distance of the Lake Michigan coastline. The two franchises don't share geography (North Side vs. South Side), leagues (National vs. American), or political allies (Chicago Mayor Richard M. Daley, like his father before him, is a diehard Sox fan; Illinois Gov. Rod Blagojevich has been a lifelong Cubs fan). But what the teams have always shared, other than a city's name and a healthy despise for one another, is decades upon decades of postseason failure. Until now. The Sox, until further notice, rule this city.

Gene Wojciechowski
October 2005

13

THE FANS

It's the best time to be a Sox fan. None of the Cubs fans can give you [bleep].

Joseph Gabriel

fan,
2005

*How many Sox fans does it take
to change a light bulb?
Well, I'll tell you.
One-half.
Why? Because they're half-lit already.*

Bob Chicoine

❖ ❖ ❖

If there is any justice in this world, to be a White Sox fan frees a man from any other form of penance.

Bill Veeck

❖ ❖ ❖

As I was growing up, I became a follower of Nellie Fox and Chico Carrasquel and Minnie Minoso and Billy Pierce and all the rest. Allegiance to the Sox was not then perceived as a form of child abuse.

Bob Vanderberg

❖ ❖ ❖

Sure I remember—Al Capone was a great baseball fan. He would come into the ballpark and people would cheer him.

Bill Veeck

I have never seen anywhere the kind of enthusiasm that was engendered in this ballpark in '77.

Bill Veeck

❖ ❖ ❖

The people, the fans, made me feel at home, completely. So after that, I figured I had a home here for a hundred years. It's true.

Minnie Minoso

❖ ❖ ❖

The people in Chicago, I knew what they wanted—and that was a winner. I met a lot of people there, had a lot of good friends there. And it was frustrating as a ballplayer not to be able to give them what they needed.

Bill Melton

❖ ❖ ❖

That city can really support, and if they can win something, man, they will go nuts.

Bill Melton
early 1980s

The crowds they got out there—I mean they were psyched. The crowd pumped us up. It was a loud crowd. It was great. Every time you'd come up there, you'd be getting a standing ovation. Every time you'd take the field, you'd get a standing ovation. It was exciting.

Oscar Gamble

I've had some great moments in a White Sox uniform, but the team hasn't been a winner. I just hope somebody can give the fans exactly what they deserve. They've been very faithful and loyal fans and they deserve a winner. We've been down for a long time. I think it's time for the White Sox to come back.

Lamar Johnson

1981

Be it tradition or inborn stubbornness, the White Sox fan has a fierce loyalty the like of which I have never experienced in my years with the Chicago Cubs, Milwaukee Brewers, Cleveland Indians, and the late, lamented St. Louis Browns.

Bill Veeck

❖ ❖ ❖

In the past, if you were born on the South Side of Chicago, you were a Sox fan from the time you saw the light of day.

Bill Veeck

❖ ❖ ❖

By the hundreds they surged toward the plane, this dedicated breed of Chicago South Siders whose loyalty and partisanship have been matched in baseball only by those rabid Brooklynites who lived and died with their beloved Bums in days long gone by.

Dave Condon
1959

Mayor Richard J. Daley, whose bungalow home on Lowe Avenue was only a pop fly from Comiskey Park, was up the landing ramp steps the instant the first of the White Sox appeared. With his family, the No. 1 White Sox fan had watched the clinching game on television; then he had sped to Midway, his enthusiasm dampened only by the misguided use of Chicago's air raid sirens, which sent thousands of citizens scurrying for refuge.

Dave Condon

on the jubilation surrounding the White Sox' pennant win in 1959, the club's first crown in 40 years. Confusing many of the Windy City's populace, air-raid sirens blared as part of the tribute when the Sox returned home in victory from Cleveland

The fans were great to me, and I loved them.

Minnie Minoso

I watched Nancy Faust (Sox organ player) play in her booth. Everyone was snapping her photo, asking her how she felt, her favorite songs, memories, and players. She was very accommodating to the fans, smiling and signing baseballs. Then I saw a tear on Nancy's cheek, followed by many more. She cried a bit and then composed herself and kept playing like the professional she is.

Gerry Bilek

on the last day at old Comiskey Park, Sept. 30, 1990

The fans feel the same way I do. . . . They want somebody to hit one out of sight. That Comiskey Park scoreboard doesn't explode for singles.

Ron Kittle

My friend Nick Torpe, rest his soul, was a Cub fan, but he was a pretty open guy. He said, "To be honest with you, I was brought up on the North Side, I always went to Cubs games, and that's probably why I'm more of a Cub fan. But Sox fans are generally more knowledgeable about the game of baseball than Cub fans are."

Don Wojcik
Sox fan since the early 1940s

It was a beautiful old ballpark, very close to the field; the fans felt a part of the action. Some were sitting behind some poles, but it was a unique place. When people came out, they knew they had had a good time.

Jeff Torborg
manager (1989–91)

This stadium held the noise better—or worse—than any other stadium. It can be intimidating for the opposing team to come in here and get rocked around a little bit and then have the whole crowd going to the "Na-Na-Hey-Hey" chant. They know they're done when that happens.

Carlton Fisk

I feel like I've found a home here. The fans have been wonderful. Can you imagine them giving me a standing ovation at the end of the season in my final appearance at the plate—when I struck out?

Dick Allen

Go Sox? At Murphy's? The place where the lone Sox pennant is hidden in a corner? This is like Mike Ditka waving a banner that says, Go Packers!

Gene Wojciechowski

on a supportive White Sox sign during the 2005 postseason outside Murphy's Bleachers, a well-known Cubs hangout

❖ ❖ ❖

In the end, this was another typical night at U.S. Cellular Field and Concert Hall, where the World Series-starved Sox crowd serenaded the Astros with a stirring rendition of "Na-Na—Na-Na-Na-Na—Hey-Hey—Goodbye."

Gene Wojciechowski

❖ ❖ ❖

I have to believe that Chicago, being the town that it is, is going to rally around a World Series winner no matter what side of town it comes from.

Stuart Scott
ESPN commentator and native Chicagoan

THE
LOCKER ROOM

It has been a long and illustrious baseball history. If there was a reverence at the passing of the old Comiskey Park and a fresh hope that characterized the birth of the new one, it will be interesting to see the cornucopia of emotions that a successful pennant race and a World Series appearance will invoke in the White Sox faithful.

Richard Whittingham
1997

Jacob Nelson Fox was born on Christmas Day, 1927. Cancer of the lymph nodes claimed his life on December 1, 1975. He was just 47 years old, my first childhood hero to die.

Bob Vanderberg

Back home in Chicago, Fire Commissioner Robert Quinn—a lifelong Sox fan—ordered the city's air-raid sirens turned on. Cub fans feared a surprise attack by the Russians. Sox fans knew better.

Bob Vanderberg

on a bizarre aspect of the citywide celebration following the Sox' AL pennant win in '59

Aw, how could he lose the ball in the sun? He's *from* Mexico."

Harry Caray

*to TV partner Bob Waller,
on second baseman Jorge Orta's
mishandling of a routine pop fly*

You're the sweetest team we've seen yet.

> **John Mayberry**
> *Kansas City Royals first baseman, to Chicago players during the first game of an Aug. 8, 1976, doubleheader that featured yet another Bill Veeck promotion: Bermuda shorts and white knee socks for the home team. Fans and the opposing Royals hooted throughout the game, though the Sox won it, 5–2. The White Sox returned to their regular uniforms for the second game—and lost.*

Carlos May may have been the only major-leaguer to wear his birth date on his jersey—May 17.

> **Dan Helpingstine**

It was Al Lopez—although he still won't admit it—who was the man behind the frozen baseballs used at Comiskey Park in the mid-'60s. It was also Al, most people think, who had groundskeeper Gene Bossard water down the infield in front of home plate to slow down hard-hit groundballs. Cold, damp baseballs—coupled with a wet, slow infield—won't do much for anyone's batting average.

Bob Vanderberg

Some players, like Ruth, Gehrig, and Shoeless Joe Jackson, defy time which ravages memory and levels reputation. The vast majority, however, no matter how highly regarded in their day, sink beneath the weight of decades, ignorance of history, and limited modern attention spans.

**Jerome Holtzman
George Vass**

Bill Melton and Dick Allen remain the only White Sox to lead in home runs, even if Albert Belle's 49 in 1998 set a new team high and Frank Thomas has surpassed 40 several times.

Jerome Holtzman
George Vass

❖ ❖ ❖

As if a White Sox home-run champion wasn't rare enough, a league leader in runs batted in is even scarcer. In fact, unique. Dick Allen, with 113 RBIs in 1972, is the only Sox player to lead the AL during its entire first century of play.

Jerome Holtzman
George Vass

❖ ❖ ❖

SEND IT FLYIN' TO THE RYAN

Left-field banner
once seen in old Comiskey Park

Jackson's wife, Katie, worked with Joe on the difficult task of signing his name for contracts and for his twice-monthly paychecks. Joe, unfamiliar with the feel of a pen in his hand, worked hard at the painstaking task of scrawling the strange-looking ten-letter signature. Eventually, Joe carried a card with his signature on it in his wallet, and when called upon to sign his name he would bring the card out and do his best to reproduce it.

David L. Fleitz
author

If they ever win something—if it really happens—I think I'm coming back. I don't care if it's only the playoffs. If they get into the playoffs, I'll be there. I won't know a soul, but I'll be there.

Bill Melton
early 1980s

I'm probably the only guy in Chicago who doesn't have the luxury of relishing in the sentimentality of what happened last season. The defeatist attitude that we'll always be Chicago's second team doesn't fly with me.

Kenny Williams
on the active off-season trading and re-signings by the Sox after winning the 2005 World Series

It's as simple as where your heart is. That's what brought me back.

Paul Konerko

on his five-year, $60 million re-signing with the White Sox in the 2005–06 off-season

The best thing of all is a winner for Chicago.

Early Wynn

15

WHITE SOX WORLD CHAMPION ROSTERS

Eighty-eight excruciating years passed between World Series crowns for Chicago's South Side team. Only their fellow city neighbors to the north have endured a longer wait for a world championship. While headliners readily abound throughout October, a world champion's roster also gathers the forgotten who toil in silence—Lee Tannehill, Jiggs Donahue, Nemo Leibold, Ziggy Hasbrook, Tadahito Iguchi, and Juan Uribe. All bore the Sox banner in Fall Classics past.

1906
93–58
World Series victors over Chicago Cubs, 4–2
Fielder Jones, *manager*

Nick Altrock, *pitcher*

George Davis, *shortstop*

Jiggs Donahue, *first base*

Patsy Dougherty, *outfield*

Gus Dundon, *second base*

Lou Fiene, *pitcher*

Ed Hahn, *outfield*

Hub Hart, *catcher*

Frank Hemphill, *outfield*

Frank Isbell, *second base*

Fielder Jones, *outfield*

Ed McFarland, *catcher*

Bill O'Neill, *outfield*

Frank Owen, *pitcher*

Roy Patterson, *pitcher*

Lee Quillen, *shortstop*

George Rohe, *third base*

Frank Roth, *catcher*

Frank Smith, *pitcher*

Billy Sullivan, *catcher*

Lee Tannehill, *third base*

Babe Towne, *catcher*

Rube Vinson, *outfield*

Ed Walsh, *pitcher*

Doc White, *pitcher*

Starters in bold

1917
100–54
World Series victors over New York Giants, 4–2
Pants Rowland, *manager*

Joe Benz, *pitcher*

Bobby Byrne,
second base

Eddie Cicotte, *pitcher*

Eddie Collins,
second base

Shano Collins, *outfield*

Dave Danforth, *pitcher*

Red Faber, *pitcher*

Happy Felsch,
center field

Jack Fournier,
pinch hitter

Chick Gandil, *first base*

Ziggy Hasbrook,
second base

Joe Jackson, *left field*

Joe Jenkins, *catcher*

Ted Jourdan, *first base*

Nemo Leibold,
right field

Byrd Lynn, *catcher*

Fred McMullin,
third base

Eddie Murphy, *outfield*

Swede Risberg,
shortstop

Reb Russell, *pitcher*

Ray Schalk, *catcher*

Jim Scott, *pitcher*

Zeb Terry, *shortstop*

Buck Weaver,
third base

Lefty Williams, *pitcher*

Mellie Wolfgang,
pitcher

2005
99–63
World Series victors over Houston Astros, 4–0
Ozzie Guillen, *manager*

Jon Adkins, *pitcher*

Brian N. Anderson, *outfield*

Jeff Bajenaru, *pitcher*

Geoff Blum, *first base*

Joe Borchard, *right field*

Mark Buehrle, *pitcher*

Jamie Burke, *first base*

Raul Casanova, *catcher*

Jose Contreras, *pitcher*

Neal Cotts, *pitcher*

Joe Crede, *third base*

Jermaine Dye, *right field*

Carl Everett, *designated hitter*

Freddy Garcia, *pitcher*

Jon Garland, *pitcher*

Ross Gload, *first base*

Willie Harris, *second base*

Dustin Hermanson, *pitcher*

Orlando Hernandez, *pitcher*

Tadahito Iguchi, *second base*

Bobby Jenks, *pitcher*

Paul Konerko, *first base*

Pedro Lopez, *second base/shortstop*

Damaso Marte, *pitcher*

Brandon McCarthy, *pitcher*

Pablo Ozuna, *third base*

Timo Perez, *outfield*

A. J. Pierzynski, *catcher*

Scott Podsednik, *left field*

Cliff Politte, *pitcher*

Aaron Rowand, *center field*

David Sanders, *pitcher*

Shingo Takatsu, *pitcher*

Frank Thomas, *designated hitter*

Juan Uribe, *shortstop*

Luis Vizcaino, *pitcher*

Kevin Walker, *pitcher*

Chris Widger, *catcher*

BIBLIOGRAPHY

Asinof, Eliot. *Bleeding Between the Lines*. New York: Holt, Rinehart and Winston, 1979.

Asinof, Eliot. *Eight Men Out: The Black Sox and the 1919 World Series*. New York: Henry Holt and Co., 1963.

Axelson, G.W. *Commy: The Life Story of Charles A. Comiskey*. McFarland Historical Baseball Library, 2; eds Marty McGee and Gary Mitchem. Jefferson, N.C.: McFarland & Co. Inc., Publishers, (1919) 2003.

Brown, Warren. *The Chicago White Sox*. New York: G.P. Putnam's Sons, 1952.

Berke, Art and Paul Schmitt. *This Date in Chicago White Sox History*. New York: Stein and Day Publishers, 1982.

Chicago White Sox: A Visual History. Prod. Timothy Roberts. Narr. Jean Shepherd. Major League Baseball Productions, 1987. 60 min.

Condon, Dave. *The Go-Go Chicago White Sox*. New York: Coward-McCann Inc., 1960.

Fleitz, David L. *Shoeless: The Life and Times of Joe Jackson*. Jefferson, N.C.: McFarland & Co. Inc., 2001.

Frommer, Harvey. *Shoeless Joe and Ragtime Baseball*. Dallas, Texas: Taylor Publishing Co., 1992.

Hageman, Bill. *Baseball Between the Wars: A Pictorial Tribute to the Men Who Made the Game in Chicago from 1909 to 1947*. New York: McGraw-Hill, 2001.

Helpingstine, Dan. *Chicago White Sox: 1959 and Beyond*. Charleston, S.C.: Arcadia Publishing, 2004.

Holtzman, Jerome and George Vass. *Baseball, Chicago Style: A Tale of Two Teams, One City*. Chicago: Bonus Books, 2001.

Kalas, Larry. *Strength Down the Middle: The Story of the 1959 Chicago White Sox*. Fort Worth, Texas: Mereken Land and Production Co., 1999.

Keown, Tim. "Glove, Actually." *ESPN the Magazine*, 7 Nov 2005: 53-54.

La Batard, Dan. "Un Par de Médias: A Pair of Sox." *ESPN the Magazine*, 21 Nov 2005: 126.

Lindberg, Rich. *Stuck on the Sox*. Evanston, Ill.: Sassafras Press, 1978.

Lindberg, Richard. *Who's on 3rd? The Chicago White Sox Story*. South Bend, Ind.: Icarus Press, 1983.

Lindberg, Richard C. *Stealing First in a Two-Team Town: The White Sox from Comiskey to Reinsdorf*. Champaign, Ill.: Sagamore Publishing, 1994.

Lindberg, Richard C. *The White Sox Encyclopedia*. Philadelphia, Pa.: Temple University Press, 1997.

Logan, Bob. *Miracle on 35th Street: Winning Ugly with the 1983 White Sox*. South Bend, Ind.: Icarus Press, 1983.

McGregor, Ed. "Daytrippers." *ESPN the Magazine*, 15 Aug 2005: 42, 44-45, 50.

Minoso, Minnie with Herb Fagen. *Just Call me Minnie: My Six Decades in Baseball*. Champaign, Ill.: Sagamore Publishing, 1994.

Morlock, Bill and Rick Little. *Split Doubleheader: An Unauthorized History of the Minnesota Twins*. Morick Inc., 1979.

Nathan, David A. *Saying It's So: A Cultural History of the Black Sox Scandal*. Urbana, Ill.: University of Illinois Press, 2003.

Old Comiskey Park: Eighty Years of Celebration, 1910-1990. Prod. T. A. Kramer. Narr. George Wendt. Grand Slam Productions Inc., 1991. 60 min.

Scott, Stuart. "Stuart Scott's Two Way: Go Lithuania!" *ESPN the Magazine*, 7 Nov 2005: 22.

The Other Side of Summer: The Wrecking of Old Comiskey Park. Dir. David Levenson. Narr. Bob Chicoine. Bougainville Productions, 1992. 37 min.

Thorn, John et al. *Total Baseball: The Official Encyclopedia of Major League Baseball*, Fifth Edition. New York: Viking Penguin, 1997.

Vanderberg, Bob. *SOX: From Lane to Fain to Zisk and Fisk*. Chicago: Chicago Review Press, 1984.

Vanderberg, Bob. *Minnie and The Mick: The Go-Go Sox Challenge the Fabled Yankee Dynasty, 1951 to 1964*. South Bend, Ind.: Diamond Communications Inc., 1996.

Vanderberg, Bob. *'59: Summer of the Sox—The Year the World Series Came to Chicago*. Sports Publishing Inc., www.SportsPublishingInc.com, 1999.

Whittingham, Richard. *The White Sox: A Pictorial History*. Chicago: Contemporary Books Inc., 1983.

Whittingham, Richard. *White Sox: The Illustrated Story*. Coal Valley, Ill.: Quality Sports Publications, 1997.

Wilbert, Warren N. and William C. Hageman. *The 1917 White Sox: Their Championship Season*. Jefferson, N.C.: McFarland & Co. Inc., Publishers, 2004.

WEB SITES:

Associated Press. "Jones' game-winner a one-hit wonder for Twins, Santana." http://sports.espn.go.com/mlb/recap?gameId=250823109, Aug. 23, 2005.

Associated Press. "Not hurtin': White Sox buy out Thomas for $3.5M." http://sports.espn.go.com/mlb/news/story?id=2214118, Nov. 4, 2005.

Associated Press. "Guillen returns to birth home a proud champion." http://sports.espn.go.com/mlb/news/story?id=2214222, Nov. 4, 2005.

Associated Press. "Guillen, Cox win manager of year awards." http://sports.espn.go.com/mlb/news/story?id=2218718, Nov. 9, 2005.

Associated Press. "Lopez was oldest living Hall of Fame member." http://sports.espn.go.com/espn/classic/obit/news/story?id=2208744, Oct. 30, 2005.

Associated Press. "Garland gets 3-year, $29 million deal from White Sox."

http://sports.espn.go.com/mlb/news/story?id=2273267, Dec. 28, 2005.

baseball-almanac.com. "Home Run Records." http://www.baseball-almanac.com/recbooks/rb_hr1.shtml.

baseball-reference.com. http://www.baseball-reference.com/teams/CHW/2005.shtml.

baseball-reference.com. http://www.baseball-reference.com/teams/CHW/1917.shtml.

baseball-reference.com. http://www.baseball-reference.com/teams/CHW/1906.shtml.

Baseball's Forgotten Man. "Quotes From Some of Robin's Team-Mates."
http://www.angelfire.com/mi/BirdWatcher/QuotesIV.html.

chicago.whitesox.mlb.com. "White Sox Broadcasters."
http://chicago.whitesox.mlb.com/NASApp/mlb/cws/history/broadcasters.jsp.

Cowley, Joe. "Cooper: Contreras will get by without Duque."
Chicago Sun-Times. http://www.suntimes.com/output/sox/cst-spt-sox16.html, December 16, 2005.

Erhardt, John. "The Week in Quotes" — October 17-23.
http://www.baseballprospectus.com/article.php?articleid=4561, October 24, 2005.

ESPN.com news services. "Konerko agrees to five-year deal with White Sox."
http://sports.espn.go.com/mlb/news/story?id=2242424, Nov. 30, 2005.

ESPN.com news services. "Vote: Are the White Sox in position to repeat?"
http://proxy.espn.go.com/chat/sportsnation/polling?event_id=1893, Nov. 30, 2005.

Jackson, Scoop. "Page 2: Pride of the South Side." ESPN.com.
http://sports.espn.go.com/espn/page2/story?page=jackson/051028, Oct. 28, 2005.National Baseball Hall of Fame. Ed Walsh.
http://www.baseballhalloffame.org/hofers_and_honorees/hofer_bios/walsh_ed.htm.

pacbellpark.com. "White Sox Coaches." http://www.pacbellpark.com/NASApp/mlb/cws/history/coaches.jsp.

Robin Quotes.
http://members.aol.com/jimmyblue3/ventura6.html.

sportsinwisconsin.com. "Wisconsin Athletic Hall of Fame, Ray Berres."
http://www.sportsinwisconsin.com/wahf/index.php?category_id=976#BerresR.

Whitfield, Paul. "Does Baines Belong in the Hall Of Fame?"
The South Sider.
http://www.thesouthsider.com/horn.html.

Wojciechowski, Gene. "Signs are everywhere for another Chicago collapse." ESPN.com.
http://sports.espn.go.com/espn/columns/story?columnist=wojciechowski_gene&id=2166625, Sept. 20, 2005.

Wojciechowski, Gene."South Side blowout no reason to break out brooms." ESPN.com.
http://sports.espn.go.com/espn/columns/story?columnist=wojciechowski_gene&id=2181188, Oct. 5, 2005.

Wojciechowski, Gene. "Guillen smokes Boston with El Duque strategy." ESPN.com.
http://sports.espn.go.com/espn/columns/story?columnist=wojciechowski_gene&id=2183947, Oct. 8, 2005.

Wojciechowski, Gene. "Even in Wrigleyville, winning White Sox rule." ESPN.com.
http://sports.espn.go.com/espn/columns/story?columnist=wojciechowski_gene&id=2197632, Oct. 19, 2005.

Wojciechowski, Gene. "Jenks hurls 'lava heat' at Bagwell in World Series Game One." ESPN.com.
http://sports.espn.go.com/espn/columns/story?columnist=wojciechowski_gene&id=2201133, Oct. 22, 2005.

Wojciechowski, Gene. "Ozzie owns Chicago, and maybe Houston, too." ESPN.com.
http://sports.espn.go.com/espn/columns/story?columnist=wojciechowski_gene&id=2202041, Oct. 25, 2005.

Wojciechowski, Gene. "There's no Series victory without Guillen." ESPN.com.
http://sports.espn.go.com/espn/columns/story?columnist=wojciechowski_gene&id=2204842, Oct. 28, 2005.

INDEX

Index

Index

Index

Miami Dolphins, 9
Miami Herald, 99
Milwaukee Brewers, 71, 149, 167, 229
Minnesota Twins, 63, 93, 103, 161, 219
Minoso, Saturnino Orestes Arrieta Armas "Minnie," 9, 22, 31, 58, 67, 69-70, 81, 99, *100*, 101, 153, 160, 163, 175, 211, 215, 226-227, 231
Minute Maid Park, 204
Miranda, Fausto, 99
Mitchem, Gary, 247
Monge, Sid, 163
Morlock, Bill, 103
Mostil, Johnny, 182, 186
Murphy, Eddie, 245
Musial, Stan, 9, 179

N

Nash, Ogden, 98
Nathan, Daniel A., 113
National Baseball Hall of Fame, 33, 82, 177, 179-180, 184-185
National League, 14, 151
Neal, Charley, 159
Negro Leagues, 81
Nelson, Amy K., 51-52, 55-56
New York Giants, 19-20, 65, 151, 154, 189, 245
New York Knicks, 41
New York World-Telegram and Sun, 78
New York Yankees, 9, 11-12, 19, 29, 34, 40, 82, 88, 112, 153, 168, 179, 189-190, 202, 217-222, 250, 253
Newark Eagles, 81
Nicholson, Dave, 42, 160-161

O

O'Neill, Bill, 244
Oakland A's, 164, 195, 219

Oklahoma State University, 178
Ordonez, Magglio, 201
Orta, Jorge, 236
Other Side of Summer: The Wrecking of Old Comiskey Park, The, 209
Ott, Mel, 90
Owen, Frank, 244
Ozuna, Pablo, 246
Ozzie Ball, 147, 204
Ozzie Factor, 145

P

Pall, Donn, 165
Patkin, Max, 24
Patterson, Roy, 17, 244
Perez, Timo, 246
Peters, Gary, 44, 140
Philadelphia Athletics, 85, 150
Phillips, Taylor, 28
Pierce, Bill Jr., 66
Pierce, Billy, 11, 21-22, 93, *94*, 96, 98, 175, 215, 218, 220-221, 226
Piersall, Jim, 156
Pierzynski, A. J., 145, 170
Pittsburgh Pirates, 142
Podsednik, Scott, 55, 58, 203, 246
Politte, Cliff, 246
Polo Grounds, 88
Power, Vic, 37
Price, Jackie, 24

Q

Quillen, Lee, 244
Quinn, Robert, 236

R

Raines, Tim, 200
Raschi, Vic, 153
Reinsdorf, Jerry, 27, 80-81, 101, 174, 180, 214
Rice, Grantland, 88
Richard, Bee Bee, 28

Richards, Paul, 13, 72-73, 131-132, 191
Rigney, Johnny, 20, 73, 153
Risberg, Swede, 116, 120, 245
Rivera, "Jungle" Jim, 31, 36, 38, 59, 66, 156, 159, 217, 221-222
Rizzuto, Phil, 34
Roberts, Timothy, 32, 91, 108, 118, 206-207
Robinson, Aaron, 21
Robinson, Eddie, 105, 153
Robinson, Floyd, 135
Robinson, Jackie, 99
Rogovin, Saul, 221
Rohe, George, 244
Romano, Honey, 156
Roth, Frank, 244
Rowand, Aaron, 56, 246
Rowland, Pants, 13, 31, 130, 245
Russell, Reb, 245
Ruth, Babe, 85, 210

S

St. Louis Browns, 15-16, 229
St. Louis Cardinals, 9, 179
San Francisco Giants, 20, 65-66, 151, 189, 245
Schalk, Ray, 117, 215, 245
Schmitt, Paul, 182
Scott, Jim, 245
Scott, Stuart, 234
Seattle Mariners, 183, 216
Shaw, Bob, 39, 59, 67-68, 140-141
Shepherd, Jean, 79, 247
Short, Ed, 185
Sievers, Roy, 25, 40, 69
Skowron, Bill "Moose," 44, 62, 135
Slaughter, Enos, 154
Slo-Mo Sox, 55

Index